HORRIBLE GEOGRAPHY

NEW EDITION

WILD Islands

'HORRIBLY GOOD' MICHAEL PALIN

Illustrated by **MIKE PHILLIPS**

SCHOLASTIC

Scholastic Children's Books,
Euston House, 24 Eversholt Street,
London NW1 1DB, UK

A division of Scholastic Ltd
London ~ New York ~ Toronto ~ Sydney ~ Auckland
Mexico City ~ New Delhi ~ Hong Kong

First published in the UK by Scholastic Ltd, 2004
This abridged edition published by Scholastic Ltd, 2016

Text copyright © Anita Ganeri, 2004, 2016
Illustrations copyright © Mike Phillips, 2004, 2016

ISBN 978 1407 17212 5

Printed in the UK by CPI Group (UK) Ltd, Croydon, CR0 4YY

2 4 6 8 10 9 7 5 3 1

The right of Anita Ganeri and Mike Phillips to be identified as the author and illustrator of this work respectively has been asserted by them in accordance with the Copyright, Designs and Patents Act, 1988.

CONTENTS

Anita Ganeri has climbed an erupting volcano, swum through shark-infested oceans and sailed round the world solo. IN HER DREAMS!

But she was born in far-away India, though she didn't realize it at the time. At school, her only interest in geography was staring out of the classroom window and working out how to escape. Since then, Horrible Geography has grown on her a bit like a mould, and she's even learned to read a map without having to turn it upside down.

Mike Phillips was born... Yippee!! No, I mean he was born in London where he grew up and up and eventually got so big he had to leave. Which is when he discovered his love of travelling, and he set off immediately to tour the world. Nearly thirty years later he has reached North Devon where he now illustrates the entire world from a sitting position.

INTRODUCTION

Is geography grinding you down? Are your geography lessons even more mind-bogglingly boring than watching the TV when it's turned off? Do you have any idea what on Earth your teacher is waffling on about?

*Roughly translated, an archipelago (ark-ee-pell-ago) is a group of islands. It's really as straightforward as that. It comes from the old Greek words for 'chief sea' and it used to mean the sea the islands were found in but it now means the islands themselves. Trouble is, horrible geographers hate to use a simple word like 'group' when they can use a tricky technical term like 'archipelago' instead. It's a mystery why they do it. You'll be able to find an archipelago on a map. (That's the big paper thing stuck on the wall behind your teacher. In case you were wondering.) By the way, the largest archipelago in the world is the Malay archipelago. It's made up of around 24,000 islands in the Pacific and Indian Oceans. Your teacher will be so gobsmacked you know this, she'll probably let you off homework for a week. You hope.

Despite the posh-sounding words and tongue-twisting terms, some bits of geography are wonderfully wild and exciting. Believe it or not. Far too exciting for a geography teacher to tell you about. Take islands, for example. Incredible islands are one of the most interesting bits of geography ever. What's more, some islands are miles from anywhere and make the perfect place to get away from it all. Ideal for relaxing on after a long, hard day staring out of the window at school. What's that? You can't wait to be off? But if you can't get to a real island, why not make one of your own? Go into the garden and chuck a truckload or two of sandy soil in the middle of the lawn. Plant a couple of clumps of palm

7

trees (tall pot plants work well for this). Dig a ditch around the edge of your island. Mind you don't fall in. Now grab the hosepipe and fill the ditch with water for the sea. (OK, so you'll need to use your imagination for this bit.) Congratulations! You're now the proud owner of your very own desert island. Well, nearly. Find yourself a deckchair and a long, cold drink and chill out.

(Warning! Ask permission first. Unless you *want* to drive your parents wild and do all the washing-up for years and years and years.)

But there's more to islands than palm trees and chilling out by the sea. Large and small, hot and cold, far-flung and closer to home, islands rear their ugly heads all over the world. In *Wild Islands*, you can…

• watch a brand-new island pop up from the sea

- live the lonely life of an island castaway

- find out why the unlucky dodo couldn't fly away

• search for a mysterious, missing island with Isla, your island-hopping guide.

ISLE SEE YOU LATER!

This is geography like never before. And it's horribly exciting. But a word of warning before you set off on your travels to find the island of your dreams. Life on a far-flung island might seem wildly exciting at first with no one to nag you to tidy your room and no little sister to nick your CDs. But being marooned in the middle of nowhere, with only a few wild goats for company, could well, er, really get your goat after a week or two. As the stranded sailor in the next chapter found out the hard way. So, before you start packing for your trip of a lifetime, why not hop over the page and check out his terrible true story.

CASTAWAY!

31 January 1709, Juan Fernandez Island, Pacific Ocean. The ship's look-out screws up his eyes and squints hard at the island in the distance. He can just make out a dark shape standing alone on the shore. But what on Earth is this strange creature? It's horribly hard to tell. The look-out shakes his head. No one lives on this isolated island. As far as he knows, at least. Perhaps he's seeing things. Lately, his eyes have been playing up. Perhaps he's getting too old for this job. But as he continues watching, the creature begins jumping up

13

and down like a mad thing, frantically waving what looks like a white rag on a stick.

WHAT THE...

The question is: who on Earth is he? And what on Earth is he doing all alone on a remote island miles from anywhere?

The look-out sounds the alarm and the ship's captain orders a rowing boat to be launched. As they row, the sailors glance nervously over their shoulders, anxious about what they'll find when they land. They don't have long to wait. Pistols at the ready, they splash on to the shore. At once, the creature rushes forward, throws up his arms and … gives the gobsmacked sailors a massive bear hug! With his matted hair, bushy beard and leathery skin burnt brown by the sun, he looks more like a wild animal than a human being. And he's dressed in filthy, ragged clothes which reek revoltingly of goat. Phwoar!

Some time later, the rowing boat returns to the ship with the wild-looking man on board. From time to time, he opens his mouth to talk but can only manage a few croaks and grunts instead of words. He hasn't talked to a soul for four long years and has almost forgotten how to speak. The captain makes him welcome and gives him something to eat and drink. Then, slowly and painfully, the mysterious stranger begins to tell his extraordinary tale…

"Ma name's Alexander Selkirk and I was born in Scotland in 1676. Ma old da was a cobbler and he wanted me tae follow in his footsteps. But ma soul wisnae really in shoes. I wanted to seek ma fortune so I ran off tae sea. (Tae tell the truth, I was in a wee spot of bother. I'd fallen oot with ma brother and gien him a good hiding. Och aye, I'd got quite a temper on me. Ma da and ma were fizzin' so I thought I'd lie low for a bit.)

"As it happens, ma luck was in. I headed doon sooth tae London and got a job on a daring expedition bound for the Sooth Seas. It was led by a salty old sea-dog and part-time pirate called Captain William Dampier. The plan was tae head for Sooth America and, on the way, capture a Spanish treasure galleon and plunder its fabulous cargo of gold. I jumped at the chance tae join. So, on 11 September 1703, the two ships in oor party – the *St George* and *Cinque Ports* – set sail from Ireland. I couldnae wait tae be off. Och, I knew the voyage would be risky and I might no make it back. But I didnae give two hoots aboot the danger. Aye, this time I thought I'd landed firmly on ma feet.

"The voyage across the Atlantic Ocean was terrible. As the weeks went by, the cranky crew got bored, then drunk, then picked fights with aibody.

The meat went mouldy, weevils ate the bread and the men dropped like flies frae scurvy*."

* Scurvy was a dreadful disease which early sailors suffered from. It was caused by not eating enough fresh fruit and veg. The awful symptoms included bad breath, gums so swollen your teeth fell out, aches and pains, blotchy skin and madness. Nice!

"By the time we reached Brazil, things had started tae turn nasty. Well nasty. Some days, there was nothing but boiled jeellyfish tae eat. Even the sight of it turned your stomach. And, tae make matters worse, Captain Dampier fell oot with aibody. Och aye, he was brave and daring all right but he had a terrible temper and he really got up ma neb. Besides, we'd been at sea for months noo, and there wisnae a single treasure ship tae be seen.

"By the time we rounded Cape Horn in January 1704, the ships were a sorry sight. We urgently needed fresh food and water so we stopped off at Juan Fernandez Island tae take on supplies. Och aye, I've been here before. It seemed like a god-forsaken place but we were desperate and at least there was plenty tae eat. We patched the ships up as best we could, then headed off again. Little did I ken I'd soon be calling this wee island home.

"Anyway, six months later (it was September 1705, if I remember right), we were back. By noo, things on board ship had gone from bad tae worse. We were doon tae half a boiled cabbage leaf a day and we were stareving.

"The ships had been badly damaged in a skirmish and were so worm-eaten they'd started tae leak. So we limped back tae Juan Fernandez tae carry oot some repairs. And that's when I really lost ma rag with the captain of ma ship, the Cinque Ports. Tae be honest, I'd never liked him either – the man was a blitherin' fool. So when he ordered us back on board, I gave him a piece of ma mind. There was no way the ship was seaworthy, I said. And if he thought I was ready tae risk ma neck on a worm-eaten bucket of rust, he'd got another think coming. I'd rather be left behind on the island than spend another second on his sinking ship!

"Me and ma big mooth! I never thought he'd go and do it. Never in ma wildest dreams. But, withoot a word, he dumped ma belongings on the shore, and sailed off. Leaving me behind!

21

I couldnae believe it. I shouted after him that I'd changed ma mind but he wisnae listening…*"

* As it turned out, Selkirk was right to abandon ship. The *Cinque Ports* sank soon afterwards and all of its crew drowned. The other ship, the *St George*, was also ditched because it was falling apart.

"For the first day or so, I stayed close tae the shore and stared oot tae sea. I was sure he'd come back for me, once he'd cooled off a bit. So I wisnae planning tae stick aroond for long. I kept a fire burning so they'd know where tae find me but I hardly slept a wink. I didnae dare close ma eyes in case I missed the ship. But as the days turned intae weeks, and the weeks intae months, the terrible truth dawned on me. I was all alone on a wee island, miles away from anywhere. And nobody knew I was there (nobody who cared, that is). What on Earth was I going tae do? As I looked around at ma new home, ma heart sank intae ma boots. The island was wild and rocky, with sheer, jagged cliffs plunging straight into the windswept sea. No the sort of place you'd pick for a holiday. At first, I thought I might as well give up there and then, and I wanted tae lie doon and die. But I pulled maself taegether. After all, it was sink or swim.

"Luckily, I had a few of ma belongings with me – ma gun, some gunpowder, a knife, a cooking pot, a Bible and ma trusty sea charts. So I built maself a hut oot of branches, thatched with grass and a bed out of wood. The place soon looked quite homely, though I say it maself. Luckily, I never went hungry. When I got fed up of crayfish, I caught some wild goats and made goat and cabbage stew. And there were plenty of roots and berries, and plums for making jam. I carved a spoon and fork oot of goat horn and used goatskins tae make clothes and a sleeping bag. The worst thing was the rats. They got everywhere and chewed holes in ma clothes and bedding. But I soon got rid of them. I kept some wild cats as rat-catchers (and they made braw pets).

"So there was plenty tae keep me busy but it was a horribly tough and lonely life. One day, when I was oot hunting, I fell off a cliff and nearly did maself in. The only thing that saved me was landing on top of a goat. I managed tae crawl back to ma hut but I was bruised black and blue and couldnae walk for days. That was a real low point. But I tried ma best tae keep ma spirits up. Every day, I carved another notch in a tree tae keep track of time.

And I often hiked up tae the mountain top tae look oot for passing ships (and it kept me fighting fit). But I'd given up any hope of being rescued. Until noo, that is…"

His voice cracking under the strain, the stranger lent forward and buried his head in his hands. A series of hacking coughs wracked his lean, bent body. After four years and four months of solitude, it was hard to believe his lonely ordeal was finally over. But he had horribly mixed feelings about leaving the island. Despite the hostile conditions, it had begun to feel like home.

Homeward bound

Two weeks later, the ship sailed out of the bay, leaving Juan Fernandez behind it. On board was Alexander Selkirk, the ship's newly appointed navigator. It took him a while to find his sea legs and he was so used to going barefoot his posh new shoes pinched his toes. And after his diet of fresh goat meat and veg, the ship's food made him horribly sick. But he didn't have time to moan. Once again, intrepid Alex found himself in the middle of an awesome adventure. The ship, called the *Duke*, was on another gold-hunting trip. But this time it was no wild goose chase. Over the next two years, the *Duke* captured several Spanish galleons and robbed their cargo of priceless treasure. By the time Alex arrived back in London, his share in all the lovely loot came to £800 – a small fortune for that time. He was rich beyond his wildest dreams.

An unhappy ending

On 30 October 1711, Alexander Selkirk finally arrived back in England again, to a hero's welcome. As he stepped off the ship, dressed in a brand-new swanskin waistcoat, crisp blue linen shirt, smart new trousers and shoes with scarlet laces (they were the height of fashion then), Alex smiled smugly to himself. He'd come a long

28

way from the cast-down castaway who ponged of old goat. A very long way indeed.

The gripping true story of his island adventures turned him into a superstar. Everywhere he went, people wanted to hear his amazing tale. For a while, Alex went back to Scotland to visit his family and have a well-earned rest. Trouble was, after all his years on the island, he couldn't stick living indoors. He built a cosy hut in the garden and sat there all day, staring out to sea. So, did Selkirk's story end happily? Did our hot-tempered hero settle down and enjoy all the fuss? Did he, heck. Before long, Alex had horribly itchy feet. He moved back to London, joined the Navy, and took to the sea again.

But that wasn't quite the end of the story. Far from it. In 1719, a sensational new book hit the shops. It was called The Life and Strange Surprising Amazing Adventures of Robinson Crusoe and it became a bestseller overnight. People went wild about it and copies sold like wildfire. The book was written by Daniel Defoe, ex-spy and sock salesman (so he knew all about itchy feet). It tells the story of a shipwrecked sailor who is stranded on a desert island. Sound familiar? Unlike our hardy hero, though, Crusoe stayed on his island for 28 years, with a man called Friday and a pet parrot called Poll for company. We don't know if the real-life Robinson Crusoe ever read the book. Unfortunately, Alex met a sticky end. He died of fever in 1721 while chasing pirates off the African coast.

A BOOK? I DIDNAE THINK OF THAT!

Wild island fact file

NAME: Juan Fernandez Island
LOCATION: Pacific Ocean
SIZE: 144 sq km (including the other islands in the group)
ISLAND TYPE: Oceanic
CAPITAL CITY: San Juan Bautista (it's the only town)
POPULATION: (today) about 800; (in Selkirk's time) 1
WILD FACTS:
• It's the peak of an underwater volcano that blew its top about four million years ago.
• It was named after ace Spanish explorer Juan Fernandez, who spotted it in 1563. He was so brilliant at navigating, people accused him of being a witch.
• In 1966 it was renamed Robinson Crusoe Island to bring in the tourists.
• The whole island's a national park because of its rare wildlife. But goats, rats or cats are banned because they eat the precious plants.

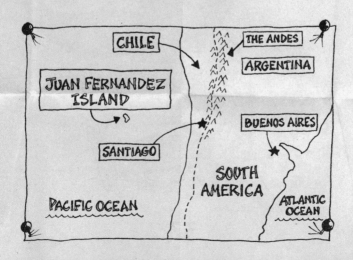

Still keen to get away from it all? Think you could really stand all that peace and quiet? (Not to mention the ravenous rats?) Well, it might be an idea to get to grips with some wild island info before you go rushing off...

INCREDIBLE ISLANDS

Ask someone to picture an island, and they'll most likely describe an idyllic desert island, with swaying palm trees and sandy beaches. Absolutely blissful. But they're not all like that. Incredible islands pop up all over the world. They range in size from colossal countries to tiny dots of rock. And they're all horribly different. True, some islands are hot and tropical – the perfect place for holidays. But some are wild and rocky, or horribly remote and cut off. And others are f-f-freezing cold and covered in ice all year round.

But don't get downhearted. You can still hope to find your dream island. With thousands of islands around, there's plenty for you to pick from. But what on Earth are islands and how on Earth did they get there?

What on Earth are islands?

Strictly speaking, an island's a chunk of land with water all around it. OK, so you don't need to be a genius geographer to work that out. But there's much more to islands than meets the eye, as you're about to sea ... sorry, see.

I THINK THIS IS AN ISLAND.

YOU DON'T SAY!

How did these incredible islands get there in the first place? Are you sitting comfortably? Long ago, there weren't any horrible geography lessons or geography teachers. (How lucky was that?) Instead, people made up stories to make sense of the world around them. Here are some of their wild theories…

• People in Hawaii and New Zealand believed the god, Maui, pulled the islands out of the sea. Mind you, he didn't mean to. He was actually on a fishing trip and  thought he'd landed a whopping great fish. Well, the story had people hooked anyway.

• In a story about Easter Island, the god, Uoke, had a terrible temper tantrum. In his rage, he prised up the Pacific islands, one by one, with his giant lever and chucked them far away. But when he got to Easter Island, his lever snapped and the grumpy god ran away, leaving Easter Island sitting all alone in the south-east Pacific.

• People in ancient Japan blamed two gods, Izanagi and Izanami, for creating their country. Legend says they stood on a rainbow in heaven and stirred the sea  with a jewel-studded spear. When they pulled the spear out, the drops of water formed the Japanese islands. Easy, peasy.

• In a story from the Philippines, the world was once made up of the sky and the sea. A giant bird spent its time flying between the two. But when the bird got tired, it couldn't find anywhere to rest, so it stirred up a quarrel between the sky and the sea. The sea was furious. It whipped up its wildest waves and hurled them up at the sky. In return, the sulky sky pelted the sea with stones. These turned into thousands of islands and that's how the Philippines came to be.

• In the Faroe Islands, people believed a gang of heavenly builders created the Earth. After a hard day's work, one builder decided to clean his fingernails. And guess what happened? The bits of grime and dirt plopped into the Atlantic Ocean and became the far-out Faroes.

So, if you believe your legends, some isolated islands came about because a builder had dirty fingernails. A likely story! But if giant fish, spiteful gods and bolshy birds weren't to blame, how on Earth did islands really rear their ugly heads?

Luckily, horrible geographers have some other island-building ideas up their sleeves.

Spotter's guide to wild islands

Can't tell one island from another? Getting your cays* confused? Don't worry. Help is at hand. Here's Isla with her very own island-spotter's guide. Why not dip in and find out about the two main kinds.

* A cay (key) is a small sandy island on a coral reef. And nothing to do with your front door key. Groan!

A)
Name: CONTINENTAL ISLANDS
Location: Close to continents
How they happen:
1. You find these islands around the edges of continents. If the sea floods a stretch of coast and cuts off the bits of high land, they stick up as islands. Many continental islands popped up when the last Ice Age ended about 10,000 years ago. Before this, gigantic glaciers covered a third of the Earth. When the weather warmed up, these slices of ice melted and colossal quantities of water poured into the sea. This made the sea level rise and huge chunks of coast were left stranded. Britain's a good example of this. Long ago, it was joined to mainland Europe and the English Channel in between was dry land you could walk across.

2. Warning! Warning! Geography lesson alert. About 200 million years ago (long before even your dear old granny was born), all the continents were one gigantic chunk of land, surrounded by an enormous sea. Over

millions and millions and millions of years, the colossal chunk split into lots of smaller bits which drifted apart ever so slowly. Some bits became the continents we have today. Other bits became islands, like marvellous Madagascar in the Indian Ocean. Until about 135 million years ago, it was part of Africa. If you get my drift.

200 MILLION YEARS AGO

135 MILLION YEARS AGO

TODAY

Earth-shattering fact

St Michael's Mount off the coast of Cornwall in southern England is a part-time island. At high tide, this tiny hill's left high and dry. But when the tide goes out, the dry seabed links it to the mainland. According to legend, the Mount is all that's left of the long-lost land of Lyonesse which was drowned by a whopping great wave. The only person to survive was a rider on a white horse. It's said you can still see his ghostly figure galloping through the surf. Spooky.

B)

Name: OCEANIC ISLANDS

Location: Far out in the odious oceans

How they happen:

These islands are horribly hot-headed. They're the tops of violent volcanoes which erupt under the sea. What happens is this: Remember the drifting continents? Well, the Earth's hard crust (that's the ground you walk on) isn't a single slab of rock. It's split into seven huge pieces (and lots of smaller ones), called plates, like the pieces of a giant's jigsaw.

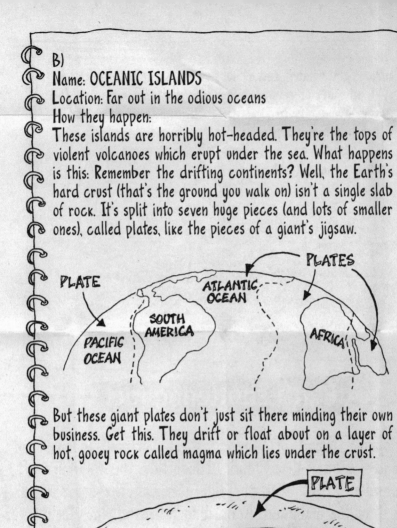

But these giant plates don't just sit there minding their own business. Get this. They drift or float about on a layer of hot, gooey rock called magma which lies under the crust.

Normally, you can't feel the plates moving, so don't worry, you won't fall off. But sometimes they get in each other's way, with explosive results. There are two places in particular where the sparks can really fly.

1. Let's split

In some places, two perishing plates of seabed start to pull apart. They pull harder and harder, until . . . . CRAAAACK! The seabed splits under the strain. Then runny, red-hot magma oozes up to plug the gap. As it hits the cold water, it cools down and turns into hard rock.

This forms long chains of massive underwater mountains and volcanoes down the middle of the oceans. The tops of some of the volcanoes poke up as islands, like Iceland and the Azores.

2. Down under

In other places, two pushy plates collide. One plate of crusty seabed is dragged down under the other and melts back into the Earth. Then it bubbles up to the surface again to build long, curving chains of islands, like Japan and Indonesia, at the edges of the oceans. Crusty geographers call them island arcs and they're seriously shaky places to live. All this pushing and shoving triggers off violent volcanic eruptions and earth-shattering earthquakes.

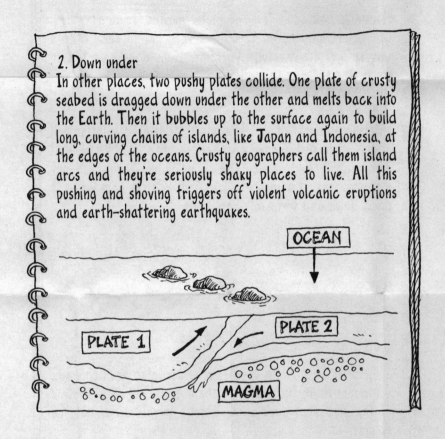

I name this island...

Look at any map of the world, and you're bound to spot some strange-sounding island names. Take the South Sandwich Islands, for starters. Or what about the barmy Belchers? See what I mean? (But at least they weren't called the Burps.) Some wild islands are named after their freaky geographical features or weird wildlife. Or the intrepid explorers who first discovered them. You get the idea. But there's more to a name than you might think. Why not try this quick quiz and work out which of these explanations are too ludicrous to be true?

1 The Canary Islands got their name from the canary bird. TRUE/ FALSE?

45

2 Easter Island got its name because it's shaped like an easter egg. TRUE/FALSE?

3 Tasmania is named after ace explorer, Abel Tasman. TRUE/FALSE?

4 The Aeolian Islands were named after wind. TRUE/FALSE?

5 Greenland got its name from its lush, green landscape. TRUE/FALSE?

ANSWER

1 **FALSE**. In fact, it's the other way round. Canary birds were named after these islands off the north-west coast of Africa because that's where they were first found. Ancient sailors thought up the islands' name because of the big, fierce muts living there. The name 'Canary'

actually comes from the Latin word for dog. Sounds barking mad.

TWEET-TWEET!

2 FALSE. Sadly, this island in the south-east Pacific has got nothing to do with yummy chocolate. Isolated Easter Island was first spotted by Europeans on Easter Day 1722 and that's how it got its name. Of course, the local people who lived there had known about the island for years. They called it "Te Pito O Te Henua" which oddly enough means 'tummy button of the world'. Wild, or what?

3 TRUE. Tasmania's an island off the south coast of Australia. It's named after ace Dutch explorer, Abel Tasman, who was the first European to reach it in 1642. Globe-trotting Tasman was a brilliant sailor and navigator and he also discovered the islands of New Zealand, Tonga and Fiji. But, strangely, he managed to sail right round Australia without seeing it. Even though it was right under his nose!

4 TRUE. But not that sort of wind! These islands of f south-west Italy are named after Aeolus, the Ancient Greek god of wind. Legend says he lived on one of these islands near Italy where he kept the wind locked up in a cave. Wild and windy weather happened when Aeolus set the wind free. Mind-blowing.

5 FALSE. Lush, green landscapes? In your dreams. The terrible truth about Greenland is that its groovy name was all just a great big con trick. Read on to find out if anyone was taken in...

Wild island fact file

NAME: Greenland
LOCATION: North Atlantic Ocean
SIZE: 2,175,600 sq km
ISLAND TYPE: Continental
CAPITAL CITY: Nuuk
POPULATION: 56,000
WILD FACTS:

• It has a horribly harsh, cold climate. Even at the height of summer, the temperature's below 10°C.
• About 80 per cent of the island is covered in a thick sheet of ice.
• The warmest bit's on the south-west coast and that's where most people live.
• Most Greenlanders live by fishing for halibut, redfish, prawns and shrimps.

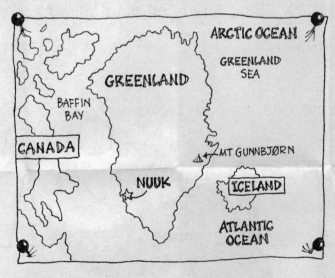

Groovy Greenland

In about AD 982, an adventurous Viking called Erik the Red went to live in Greenland. Actually, he didn't have much choice. Back home in Iceland, he'd killed two men and been banished as punishment. (By the way,  Erik got his own name because of his red hair and beard, and probably his terrible temper.)

With no one to pick a fight with, Erik soon got horribly lonely and bored. But how on Earth was he going to persuade any

other Vikings to come and live on this freezing cold island with him?

Then enterprising Erik had a brilliant idea. Never mind the immense icebergs. Forget the gruesome glaciers. He called the island Greenland and pretended it was lovely, warm, and … well, beautifully lush and green.

And, believe it or not, his trick worked a treat. Greenland sounded like such a cool place to live that people were green with envy. About 500 Vikings packed their bags and set off from Iceland to join him. Bet they were shivering with all the excitement.

Despite the chilly conditions, the tough-nut Vikings lived on Greenland for years. Once the shock wore off, that is. They built snug houses from stone, wood and turf, planted  crops and kept cattle, goats and sheep (which they brought with them from home).

But about 500 years later, the Vikings disappeared. What happened is still a mystery. But horrible history experts reckon the weather

suddenly took a turn for the worse. The Vikings' clothes weren't warm enough and the cold weather killed off their crops so the Vikings either froze or starved to death.

It's a pity the Vikings didn't ask the local Inuit people for help. After all, they'd lived in Greenland for thousands of years before the Vikings got there. And they knew all about coping with the cold. The Inuit moved from place to place, hunting seals and other wild animals for food. And they used the fur and skins to make toasty warm clothes. Most modern Greenlanders are descended from the Inuit. But today their lives have changed. Most of them now live in towns and settlements with all the latest mod cons. They have to work hard to stop their traditional lifestyle and language from dying out.

HMMM...

TEACHER TEASER

Feeling brave? Go on, try this experiment. While your teacher's having her tea-break, knock gently on the staff-room door and ask this question.

Sounds like it should have a simple answer, doesn't it? But some bits of horrible geography are so confusing even teachers can't agree.

ANSWER

The answer is yes ... and no! Some horrible geographers agree that Greenland's gigantic but reckon the world's largest island is actually awesome Australia which is three times as big. Others say that though Australia's bigger (and surrounded by sea), it really counts as a continent and not an island at all. So who do you believe?

Wild islands top ten

While your teachers are still squabbling, here's Isla with a handy map to show you where on Earth the top ten biggest islands are and the type of island you might find yourself stranded on. (We've counted Greenland as number one.)

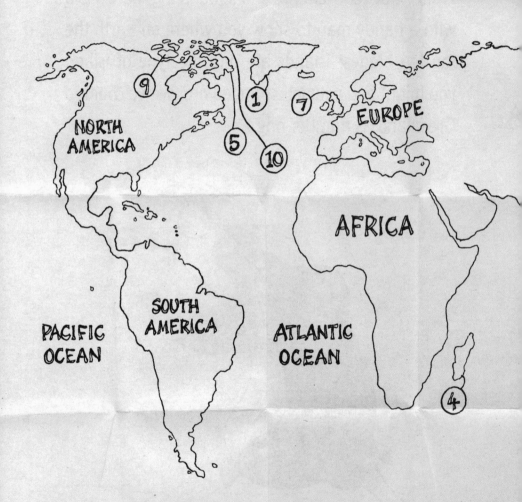

NORTH
AMERICA

EUROPE

AFRICA

SOUTH
AMERICA

PACIFIC
OCEAN

ATLANTIC
OCEAN

ASIA

PACIFIC
OCEAN

INDIAN
OCEAN

AUSTRALIA

| KEY | C = CONTINENTAL |
| | O = OCEANIC |

1. **GREENLAND** C
   (2,175,600 SQ KM)
2. **NEW GUINEA** C
   (821,400 SQ KM)
3. **BORNEO** O
   (755,000 SQ KM)
4. **MADAGASCAR** C
   (587,051 SQ KM)
5. **BAFFIN** C
   (507,451 SQ KM)
6. **SUMATRA** O
   (443,066 SQ KM)
7. **GREAT BRITAIN** C
   (229,957 SQ KM)
8. **HONSHU (JAPAN)** O
   (227,898 SQ KM)
9. **VICTORIA** C
   (217,291 SQ KM)
10. **ELLESMERE** C
    (196,236 SQ KM)

Horrible Health Warning

Pick your wild island carefully. Living miles away from anywhere's all very well but you can't just pop to the shops if you run out of crisps. Especially if you end up on isolated Bouvet Island. You'll be alone in the stormy South Atlantic, about 1,700 kilometres from the nearest land. And that's icy Antarctica where nobody lives anyway. Perfect if you like penguins for company.

FLAMING ISLANDS

So are you any closer to finding the wild island that's right for you? Or are you one of those people who think islands are just boring lumps of rock that sit around in the sea all day? If the incredible islands you've seen so far have left you cold, it might be time to turn up the heat. Luckily, you've come to the right place. This whole chapter's packed with earth-shattering info about odious oceanic islands. But be careful. After all, many of these flaming islands are violent volcanoes. They're terribly hot-tempered and have a horrible habit of blowing their tops. So you might not get much peace and quiet but you'll get plenty of thrills and spills. Feeling brave? You'll need to be. Things are about to get horribly exciting.

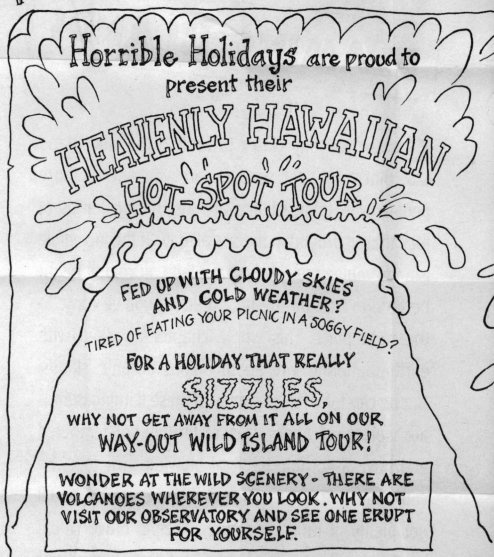

Horrible Holidays are proud to present their

HEAVENLY HAWAIIAN HOT-SPOT TOUR

FED UP WITH CLOUDY SKIES AND COLD WEATHER? TIRED OF EATING YOUR PICNIC IN A SOGGY FIELD?

FOR A HOLIDAY THAT REALLY **SIZZLES,** WHY NOT GET AWAY FROM IT ALL ON OUR WAY-OUT WILD ISLAND TOUR!

WONDER AT THE WILD SCENERY - THERE ARE VOLCANOES WHEREVER YOU LOOK. WHY NOT VISIT OUR OBSERVATORY AND SEE ONE ERUPT FOR YOURSELF.

RELAX ON PALM-FRINGED BEACHES - DON'T BE PUT OFF BY THE BLACK SAND. IT'S MADE FROM VOLCANIC ROCK. SO MIND YOU DON'T SINGE YOUR TOES

MAKE AN OFFERING TO PELE, THE FIRE GODDESS - SOME FLOWERS OR FRUIT WILL DO. THE STORY GOES THAT PELE'S TEMPER TANTRUMS CAUSED THE ISLANDS TO ERUPT FROM THE SEA. WHAT A HOT HEAD!

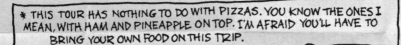

BOOK YOUR PLACE TODAY!

WHAT ONE SATISFIED CUSTOMER SAID:

PHEW! WHAT A SCORCHER. IT'S THE HOTTEST HOLIDAY I'VE BEEN ON FOR YEARS. A FLAMING LOVELY TRIP.

* THIS TOUR HAS NOTHING TO DO WITH PIZZAS. YOU KNOW THE ONES I MEAN, WITH HAM AND PINEAPPLE ON TOP. I'M AFRAID YOU'LL HAVE TO BRING YOUR OWN FOOD ON THIS TRIP.

Island hot-spots

The idyllic islands of Hawaii in the Pacific Ocean are oceanic islands like those of Iceland and Japan. And like these wild islands, they're the tops of vast volcanoes that tower up from the seabed. But they're formed in a different way. Horrible geographers called them hot-spot volcanoes because of the way the islands grow. And in case you're wondering what on Earth they're talking about, here's the inside story of hot spots…

1 A stream of magma rises up from deep inside the Earth. It punches a hole in the seabed crust above it to form a horrible hot spot. The

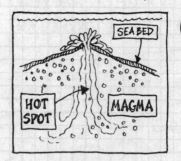

hot spot under Hawaii is about 320 kilometres wide

and lies about 60 kilometres under the sea.

2 As the magma bubbles up through the hole, it turns into solid rock. This builds up, and up and up, and forms a violent volcano. If the volcano grows tall enough, it pokes up as a hot-spot island. But don't hold your breath. This takes millions and millions of years.

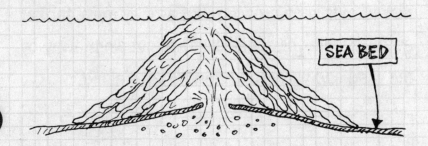

3 Over the years, the hot spot stays rooted to the spot while the plate above it drifts slowly across it. As it does so, the magma punches brand-new holes in the seabed to make brand-new volcanoes. It's a bit like being on a gigantic volcano conveyor belt.

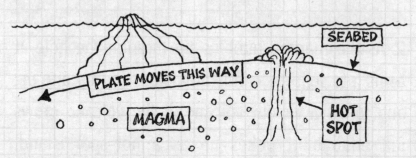

4 As long as the volcanoes stick close to the hot spot, there's plenty of magma to make them erupt and new islands keep growing. But as they move further away, the vile volcanoes die. They get worn away by the wind and waves and slowly start sinking.

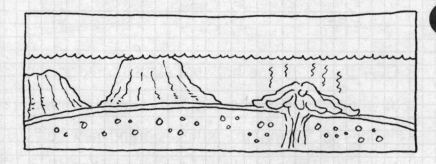

5 Still, it isn't all doom and gloom. As one old island disappears, a new one pops up above the hot spot. While you're reading this Horrible Geography book, a new Hawaiian island called Loihi's already bubbling away under the sea and it's already almost 3 kilometres tall. Horribly excited geographers have been sending down submarines fitted with cameras to check on little Loihi's progress. But they'll have a very long wait. It'll take at least another 60,000 years for Loihi to poke its head above the sea.

Wild island fact file

NAME: Hawaii
LOCATION: Pacific Ocean
SIZE: 28,412 sq km
ISLAND TYPE: Oceanic
CAPITAL CITY: Honolulu
POPULATION: about 1,360,000
WILD FACTS:

• It's a chain of 132 islands, stretching for 2,450 kilometres.

• There are eight large islands and 124 titchier ones. Hawaii's also the name of the biggest island, though the locals call it "Big Island" so they know which is which.

• The islands range in age from 700,000 to 28 million years old. The oldest islands are the ones furthest away from the hot spot.

• Kilauea, on Hawaii, is the world's most active volcano. It's been erupting non-stop since 1983.

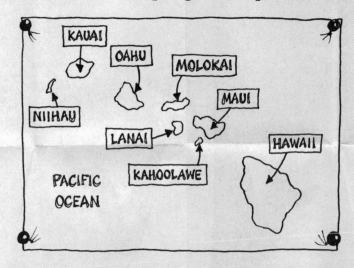

TEACHER TEASER

Want to put your geography teacher in the hot seat?
Make a puzzled face, and ask this pointed question.

Now watch your teacher try to keep his cool.

Your teacher will probably tell you it's mighty Mount Everest in the Himalayas in Asia. But they'd be woefully wrong and way off the mark. In fact, the tallest mountain on Earth is massive Mauna Kea, a freaky peak on Hawaii. At a staggering 10,203 metres tall from base to tip, this vast volcano easily beats Everest (at a measly 8,848 metres tall) into second place. Of course, Mauna Kea has a head start. Over half of this vast volcano lies underwater but its top pokes out of the sea to form part of heavenly Hawaii.

I DIDN'T KNOW HAWAII WAS THIS TALL. I'M SCARED OF HEIGHTS!

Sink or swim

So you see, volcanic islands don't hang around for ever. But there's no need to panic. An island can take millions and millions of years to sink so you don't have to start swimming yet. But do these sinking islands vanish without trace, like your long-lost geography homework? No, not quite. Some of them leave another kind of island behind which is called an atoll. Getting that sinking feeling? Finding things hard to understand? Don't worry.

To clear up the confusion, we've called in Isla, our island expert...

What on Earth are atolls?

So coral's a kind of rock, is it?

Nope. Coral's made by tiny sea creatures, closely related to sea anemones and jellyfish. They live together in gigantic groups, millions and millions strong. These squishy creatures build hard, stony cases to protect their soft bodies. A reef's built from the empty cases left behind when the creatures die. And a ring of reefs makes an atoll.

CORAL

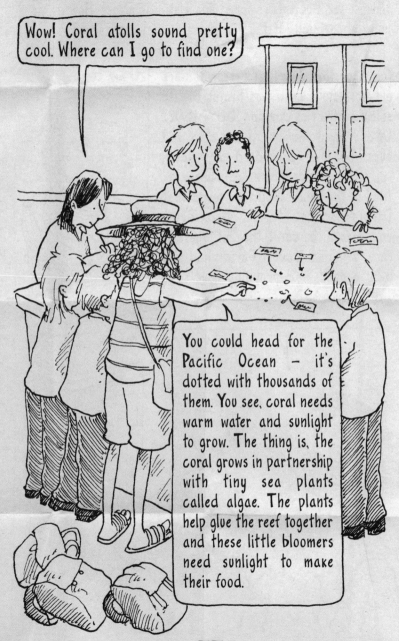

77

Hmm, I see. But there's something I still don't get. How do we know about atolls, if the volcanoes have already sunk?

Good question. The first person to work out how atolls grow was brainy British scientist, Charles Darwin (1809-1882). Of course, at the time, it was all a wild guess. But over a hundred years later, scientists were drilling holes in Enewetak Atoll in the Pacific and they found that Darwin had got it right. Deep down, underneath the coral, they hit layers of rock. Volcanic rock. If Darwin had still been around, he'd probably have said, "Atoll-d you so."

But in case you're thinking of getting to know your fabulous flaming island better, remember it could turn out to be a killer. It's true. Even if a violent volcano looks long-dead, it could still blow its top at any time. You won't just get a lovely suntan – you'll be burnt to a bloomin' crisp.

The incredible exploding island

The Sunda Strait, Indonesia, 27 August 1883.

The day dawned like any other over the Sunda Strait between the Indonesian islands of Java and Sumatra. But this was to be no ordinary day. It was a day people all over the world would never forget. Krakatoa, a tiny volcanic island in the Strait, had been slumbering away gently for 200 years. In fact, many people thought the volcano must be extinct. Now, after months of minor explosions, this sleeping giant was stirring again. And at 10 a.m. on 27 August, Krakatoa finally erupted and blew itself to smithereens.

For three months before the eruption, people living on the nearby islands noticed ominous rumbling sounds and plumes of smoke – sure signs the volcano was about to erupt. And passing ships reported having to dodge enormous chunks of pumice* which were choking up the sea.

* Pumice is a kind of volcanic rock and amazingly it's light enough to float on the sea. That's because it's full of holes, left when bubbles of gas go pop. Some people use pumice stones to rub stubborn hard skin off their smelly feet!

But nobody expected what came next. By the afternoon of 26 August, the rumblings had got louder and louder, and turned into deafening explosions. A huge black cloud of hot ash and gas hung above the sea and brilliant bolts of lightning flashed across the sky. The captain of a passing ship thought he was sailing into a storm. But instead of rain, a shower of volcanic ash poured down on his ship. Here's his eyewitness account which he wrote in his logbook:

The ash shower is becoming heavier and is mixed with fragments of pumice stone. The lightning and thunder became worse and worse. Fireballs fell on the deck and burst into sparks . . . and we heard fearful rumblings and explosions. At 2 a.m. on Monday, the 27th, a layer of ash, a metre thick, was lying on the ship. I had continually to pull my legs out of the ashy layers to prevent them from being buried. The ashes were hot . . . and burned large holes in our clothing and the sails.

But worse was to come. Eight hours later, at 10 a.m., all hell broke loose. With a gigantic BANG!, the whole island blew itself apart. When the dust finally settled and the skies cleared, it was found that two-thirds of Krakatoa had slumped into the sea.

Five freaky facts about Krakatoa

1 The sound of the eruption was the loudest that's ever been heard. People on Rodriguez Island 4,800 kilometres away in the Indian Ocean mistook it for the sound of gunfire and thought they were under attack. And it woke people up in Australia, 3,200 kilometres away.

2 The shock triggered off a monster wave called a tsunami (soo-na-mee). It was a staggering 40 metres tall – that's as high as a ten-storey building. This killer wave swept over the nearby islands of Java and Sumatra, with deadly results. Some 163 villages were washed away and 36,000 people drowned.

3 The eruption blasted a colossal cloud of hot ash, fire and rock 80 kilometres into the sky. Showers of ash rained down on ships up to 6,000 kilometres away. (Bet they wondered what on Earth was going on.)

4 So much awesome ash and dust was belched out into the air, it blotted out the sun. For the next ten years, temperatures around the world dropped by 1°C. It doesn't sound much but it made winters much nippier. The dust also caused such bright sunsets that some people thought there was a fire and called out the fire brigade.

5 But the story didn't end there. In 1927, locals noticed the sea where Krakatoa stood had begun to bubble and steam again. Two years' later, a brand-new island popped up. This flaming island was called Anak Krakatoa which means 'child of Krakatoa'. So far, Krakatoa Junior's been sleeping peacefully. But don't be fooled. One thing to remember about volcanoes is that they're horribly unpredictable. So watch this space.

Earth-shattering fact

It's not every day an island gets mistaken for a submarine. But that's exactly what happened to Ferdinandea, an underwater volcano in the Med. In 1987, a United States warplane decided it was an enemy sub and dropped a bomb on it. Talk about dropping a bombshell. This wild island last surfaced in August 1831, off the coast of Sicily. Amazingly, six months later, it was gone again.

Wild island birthday

Picture the scene. You're happily messing about on the sea, hoping to catch a couple of fish for your tea. When suddenly the sea around your boat starts to bubble and hiss. Next thing you know, there's a brand-new island right in front of your eyes. Sounds too wild to be true? Well, that's exactly what happened to some wild-eyed Icelandic fishermen in 1963. Luckily, our *Daily Globe* reporter was on hand to record this earth-shattering event.

The Daily Globe

FISHERMEN IN FIRE ISLAND SHOCK

The shell-shocked crew of a fishing boat was recovering last night after a routine fishing trip threw up the surprise of their lives.

Early yesterday morning, the men were fishing off the south coast of Iceland.

At first, everything seemed normal. But not for long.

"The first thing we noticed was the terrible smell," one of the men told our reporter. "It was horrible – like rotten eggs. And the sea started to get very choppy, even though there wasn't any wind. It was terrifying."

As the men watched, a huge cloud of black smoke billowed up from the sea. At first, they thought a boat was on fire. But when they got closer, there was no boat to be seen. Instead, an extraordinary sight met their eyes. Another man took up the tale:

"The smoke was coming from the sea," he said. "The water was boiling and bubbling, and went a very weird shade of red. In all my years of fishing, I'd never seen anything like it. Then huge lumps of ash and rock started spurting up into the air.

"We decided to phone the local radio station to let them know the score. Then we were outta there!"

By mid-afternoon, the

plume of smoke could be seen in the Icelandic capital, Reykjavik, 120 kilometres away. Then the fireworks began. Every few seconds, the sea exploded, blasting lava bombs into the air. As they fell back into the sea, they burst into huge white balls of steam.

Excited children from local schools were given the afternoon off to watch.

"It was brilliant," one lad told us. "And best of all, we missed double geography."

According to our geography expert, Dr Cliff Top, the flabbergasted fishermen have had a once-in-a-lifetime experience. They've witnessed a volcanic island being born along the Mid-Atlantic Ridge (a great split in the seabed where red-hot magma bubbles up and which has already built nearby Iceland). And once they've got over the shock, we're sure they'll look on the bright side. The new island's already been given a name. Locals have called it Surtsey, after an ancient Icelandic god of fire. So, Happy Birthday, Surtsey,

from all of us at the *Daily Globe!* Judging by what we've seen so far, things should really heat up over the next few days. And you won't miss a thing. With our exclusive coverage, readers of the *Daily Globe* can keep bang up to date with all the red-hot developments.

Over the next two years, Surtsey grew quickly until it measured about 2.5 square kilometres. But it was still bare and covered in thick, black ash. Surely nothing could live on that wild wasteland? But just a few months later, scientists were astonished to see the first plants growing. They'd sprouted from seeds carried there by birds or the wind. Since then, more seeds, birds and insects have followed, and the island's wildlife is flourishing.

And if it's wild island wildlife you're after, why not follow me into the next chapter? It's all about island animals, and some of them are seriously strange. Forget boring pet hamsters and guinea pigs. Depending on which island you choose to live on, you're more likely to meet tortoises the size of cars and larger-than-life lizards with bad breath. Now, don't go wandering off...

ISLAND WILDLIFE

Islands are amazing places for watching wildlife. Why? Well, some of them are so far-out and isolated, the plants and animals that live there don't live ANYWHERE ELSE ON EARTH. But hang on a minute, you might say, some of these islands are miles from anywhere and surrounded by thousands of miles of sea. So how on Earth did all these horribly hardy and hard-to-find plants and animals get there in the first place?

See if you can work out the answer to this puzzling problem with this quick quiz.

c) They hitch a lift on a bird. TRUE/FALSE?

d) They float across on logs. TRUE/FALSE?

e) They walk across on a bridge of dry land. TRUE/FALSE?

Unbelievably, they're all TRUE.

a) Some plants have such small, light seeds, even a slight puff of wind can pick them up and blow them thousands of kilometres away. If the seeds land on a suitable island, they'll start to sprout. And that way there's plenty of food and shelter for the animals which arrive later. Bloomin' marvellous, eh?

b) Heavyweight seeds like coconuts are hollow so they can drift in the water for weeks until they wash up on an island shore and sprout into palm trees. Their thick, hairy shells help them to float and stop them getting waterlogged. Talk about tough nuts.

c) Some seeds are covered in glue or have tiny hooks for sticking onto passing birds. They stick to the birds' beaks and feathers, and even to the mud on their feet. When the birds fly off to an island, they take the seeds with them. So you

could say these sticky seeds get off to a flying start. Many birds also like to scoff fruit for tea, then the seeds plop out in their poo. Sounds disgusting but if the seeds land on an island, they stand a good chance of sprouting into lovely new trees.

d) It's true. Hardy sailors like snails, millipedes, spiders and even snakes hitch lifts on rafts of floating logs and driftwood which rivers wash into the sea. These peckish passengers spend most of the journey nibbling away on all the bits of plants and veg. Good job they don't get seasick.

e) On continental islands, you usually get the same kinds of plants and animals you find on the mainland. This is because they pootled across when the sea level was lower and the two places were joined by dry land. Then the sea level rose, leaving them stranded in their new home.

Earth-shattering fact

The giant coco-de-mer palm trees from the Seychelles grow the biggest nuts on Earth. These beauties weigh as much as 50 normal-sized coconuts. No wonder when people first came across them, they went absolutely nuts. They reckoned the nuts had magical powers. They carved the shells into enormous cups, which they believed could turn deadly poison into a harmless, refreshing drink. There was just one tiny problem with this nutty idea. By the time you'd taken a sip or two to test this out, chances are you'd be a goner anyway.

WHAT A NUTTER!

Wild island safari

The best place to watch island animals is in the wild, of course. Luckily for you there are still a few places left on our very own Horrible Geography Wild Island Safari. It's a once-in-a-lifetime opportunity you won't want to miss, even if things can get pretty wild and woolly, and you'll need to be feeling brave. What's that? Scared stiff of spiders? Worried you'll end up as a wild animal's lunch? Don't panic – you'll be in very good hands. Our gutsy guide for this thrilling tour is none other than Isla's Uncle Rocky. And yes, those *are* bite marks on his leg. But they're healing up nicely, thanks.

Hello, folks, Rocky here, welcoming you on our wild island safari. A wild old time is guaranteed, you can take my word for it. But before we get going, there are a couple of things you should know. Now, most of the wild animals you're going to meet wouldn't hurt a fly. In fact, they're horribly shy and sensitive and used to having their wild islands to themselves. So please don't make too much noise or move suddenly. (Yes, madam, you can run away. But for goodness' sake, do it slowly.) We don't want them scarpering, do we, before you've had a chance to take some snaps? Right then, everyone ready? OK, let's be off.

1. GIANT TORTOISE

HABITAT: Galápagos Islands.

APPEARANCE: Er, like a giant, and I mean GIANT tortoise. It can grow 1.5m long and weigh a quarter of a tonne. Imagine having one of these outsized reptiles rummaging around at the bottom of your garden!

These whoppers were once so common, visitors claimed they could use them as giant stepping-stones and walk long distances across their backs. Without touching the ground once! But early sailors killed so many for their meat, they almost wiped them out. Get this. The sailors bundled them into the ships' holds, **STILL ALIVE** and turned upside down on their backs, for weeks on end. They said it kept the meat nice and fresh, like a sort of tortoise takeaway. Horribly cruel, I know. Especially as these giants can live to the ripe old age of 200 in the wild.

What's that, sir? No, we don't allow visitors to feed them. They normally eat almost any kind of fruit or veg but they're not really fussy. These beauties would eat you out of house and home, given half a chance. Including your tent and clothes. Oh watch out, madam, hold on to your hat.... Oops, too late!

2. AYE-AYE

HABITAT: Madagascar.

APPEARANCE: Like the winner of a bits-of-leftover-animal competition. Except, amazingly enough, this little fella's for real. It's about the size of a pet cat, with ears like a bat, long front teeth like a rabbit, and a big, bushy tail like a fox.

Yes, I know it's not everyone's cup of tea but this little fella's my favourite. It's a kind of animal called a lemur which only lives in Madagascar. But ssshhh! Please keep your voices down. Aye-ayes are seriously shy and secretive and only come out at night. The rest of the time they like to sit in a tree and hide. So we might be here for some time. While we're waiting, I'll fill you in on some strange-but-true details. The aye-aye's freaky features include very long, bony middle fingers that look like dead twigs. Have you twigged what they're used for? Yes, they're for stabbing insect grubs hidden under the tree bark. Sadly, there aren't many aye-ayes left. Their forest homes have been cut down and local people kill them because they think they've got evil powers.

So wakey, wakey, everyone! We don't want you nodding off and missing it now, do we?

Wild island fact file

NAME: Madagascar
LOCATION: Indian Ocean
SIZE: 587,051 sq km
ISLAND TYPE: Continental
CAPITAL CITY: Antananarivo
POPULATION: 23,812,681
WILD FACTS:
• It's the fourth biggest island in the world.
• Until about 135 million years ago, it was part of Africa. Then it split off from the mainland and became an isolated island.
• It's a treasure chest of nature. Three-quarters of the island's plants and animals aren't found anywhere else on Earth.
• In the 16th and 17th centuries, it was a favourite stopping-off place for treasure-seeking pirates.

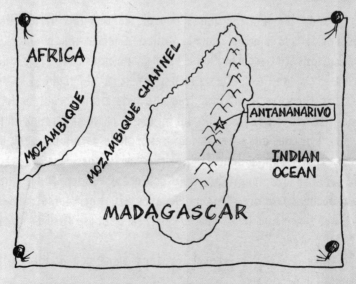

3. BIRD OF PARADISE.

HABITAT: NEW GUINEA/AUSTRALIA

APPEARANCE: About the same size as a magpie but much more dashing. The males have long brilliantly coloured feathers on their heads and tails. When people first saw these dazzling birds, they couldn't believe their eyes. They reckoned they were so beautiful they must have come from paradise. And that's how they got their heavenly name.

HORRIBLE HABITS:

Now, cameras ready, everyone. You're in for a real treat. These little beauties love showing off their finery. Just like some humans dress up in their best clothes on special occasions, male birds of paradise dress up to attract a mate. They sit in a tree, strutting their stuff and showing off their gorgeous feathers. No wonder passing females go weak at the knees. And the bird with the most dazzling display usually gets the girl.

This larger-than-life lizard's got frightful feeding habits. It mostly eats chickens, pigs and goats and doesn't mind if they're alive or dead. Here's what the dragons do. They lie in wait in the forest for their lunch to pass by. Then they pounce, grab it by the leg, and rip it to shreds. Very nasty! What's more, dragons can open their mouth wide enough to gulp a goat down — WHOLE! Now that's what I call jaw-dropping.

Are you feeling all right, sir? Yes, you at the back. You're looking rather green.

HORRIBLE HEALTH WARNING

If you're going dragon-spotting, keep your distance. Whatever you do. Apart from terrible table manners, these monstrous lizards have got horribly bad breath. In fact, it's so revolting it makes your stinky socks smell like a bunch of roses. Phwoar! What a whiff. And try your best not to get bitten. The dragon's spit's so fearfully foul and poisonous, wounds can fester and take weeks to heal.

Well, that's all we've got time for, folks. Thank you for coming and I hope you've enjoyed the trip. What's that, sonny? Er, no, I wouldn't advise keeping a Komodo dragon as a pet. Imagine trying to take it for a walk. You'd be much better off with a dog. Now, if no one's got any more questions, I'll be off. I don't know about you but my feet are killing me and I'm dying for a cup of tea.

Dead as a dodo: the bird that bit the dust

Unfortunately, there's one island animal you won't be able to spot on any safari. In fact, you can only see it today in pictures in books and stuffed in a museum. That's because the last one bit the dust in 1680. So while you're putting your feet up and sipping your cuppa, here's a story that'll bring a tear to your eye. It's the tragic true tale of the dodo, a bird which sadly has gone down in history for being dead. Long dead.

For thousands of years, the dodo lived happily on the sunny island of Mauritius in the Indian Ocean. It looked like a (very) plump pigeon  with fluffy, grey feathers. It had short yellow legs, stubby little wings and a huge yellow-and-green hooked beak. And a clump of curly white feathers stuck up in a tuft at the end of its tail. OK, so this bizarre-looking bird was no oil painting and it wasn't going to win any beauty contests. But it was gentle-natured and harmless, and made friends with everyone. Then everything changed. One minute, the dodo was waddling about merrily, minding its own business. The next, its world had been turned upside down by the arrival of horrible humans. Here's what happened…

In the 16th century, sailors from Holland and Portugal landed on Mauritius to stock up their ships with supplies. They couldn't believe their luck when they spotted the dodos. These bumbling birds were so trusting, they walked right up to the sailors. And so the sailors … clubbed them to death. Thousands of dodos were killed for their meat (even though it was horribly tough to chew). And to make matters worse, the rats and cats the sailors brought with them on their ships scoffed the dodos' eggs and chicks.

Of course, you can't blame the dodos. They were just too bloomin' tame and trusting. Trouble was, they'd lived in splendid isolation for so long, they'd got used to having the place to themselves. And, like lots of other island birds, they couldn't fly so they couldn't get away. They'd never needed to, you see. They hadn't an enemy in the world so they didn't need to escape. Besides, flying used up loads of energy so there was no point getting in a flap about it.

Sadly, sniff, around 150 years later, there were no dodos left. The desperately unlucky dodo was well ... dead as a dodo. Now where's that hanky?

Recently, a scientist in Mauritius noticed something strange about a type of tree. For a start, there were only thirteen of this particular tree left. And secondly, they were all over 300 years old. No new trees had sprouted since the late 1600s – exactly the same time the dodo became extinct. Were the two things connected? Or was it just coincidence? The scientist was baffled, then he made a startling discovery. It turned out the dodo used to eat the tree's fruit, then squirted out the seeds in its poo. And if they hadn't gone through the dodo's guts, the seeds simply wouldn't sprout. The tree looked like it was for the chop. But then the scientist had a brainwave. He fed some fruit to a turkey (the closest thing to a dodo he could find) and waited for the turkey to you-know-what. And thanks to his seedy experiment, a new tree was soon sprouting!

I FEEL LIKE A RIGHT TURKEY!

A ground-breaking journey

Another scientist who was wild about islands was brilliant Charles Darwin (1809–1882). Remember his ingenious ideas about coral atolls? When he left school, Charles went off to university to study medicine but he wasn't much good at passing exams. So he trained to be a clergyman but he soon got bored of that, too. He preferred to spend his time going for long walks in the countryside and collecting beetles and bugs.

When Charles was just 22 years old, something happened that changed his life. He got a job as a ship's naturalist on a five-year voyage around the world to study wildlife. On the way, the ship sailed round South America and stopped off at the Galápagos Islands. And there Darwin made a daring discovery that changed the history of science.

Here's how he might have described the voyage in a letter home to his cousin.

HMS Beagle, off the Galápagos Islands, October 1835

My dear Emma,
    I hope this letter finds you well. I'm sorry I haven't written for ages but I've been pretty busy, you see. And since we left London, I've also been horribly seasick. I'm feeling a bit better now. Oh, er, hang on, spoke too soon...

NORTH AMERICA

SOUTH AMERICA

GALÁPAGOS ISLANDS

    Sorry about that. Anyway, where was I? Oh yes. We've been at sea for four years now and what a voyage it's been. Despite feeling sick all the time, I still can't believe my luck. The ship's really started to feel like home. I have to share a cabin with Captain Fitzroy. It's a bit of a squeeze, to say the least. Just lately, Captain F's been complaining about all my clutter (he means my precious plant and animal specimens). He says there isn't room to swing a cat in the cabin, let alone put up his hammock. And he's always stubbing his toe on piles of fossils and old bones. Clumsy, I call it. But, apart from that, we get on swimmingly.

We sailed down to South America, making lots of stops on the way. It was so exciting. While Captain F. stayed on board and made charts of the coast, I had plenty of time to go ashore and collect lots more creepy-crawlies. So far, so good. But when we sailed around treacherous Cape Horn, the weather took a turn for the worse. A terrible storm blew up and the sea got horribly choppy. Even thinking about it makes me feel ... sorry, back in a tick.

But the best bit of the trip so far was stopping off at the Galápagos Islands where we spent five unforgettable weeks. What an extraordinary place it is. It's full of amazing animals that you don't find anywhere else on Earth. For example, there's

ME lions and birds. I got loads of specimens. (Though goodness knows where I'm going to put them.) And I even got to ride on a giant tortoise, though it was a bit wobbly and I almost fell off. It was only later at supper that I suddenly had a thought. Actually, we were tucking into roast tortoise at the time and it was the empty tortoiseshell that tipped me off.

You see, you get tortoises on each of the islands. But each type of tortoise has a slightly different-shaped shell. And it's the same with the finches. They're quite drab little birds and they crop up everywhere. But each island has its own version, with a slightly different-shaped beak. I reckon it must be something to do with what they eat but I'm not sure. It's food for thought, anyway. Oh dear, I wish I hadn't mentioned food. It's made me feel quite queasy...

See you soon.
Love from your cousin,
Charles xxx

Fussy finches match up

So Darwin was all of a dither. How could he test his theory out? Perhaps you can help him by matching each of these fussy finches' beaks to a favourite supper-time snack?

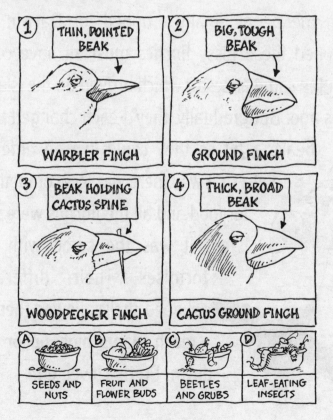

1. THIN, POINTED BEAK — WARBLER FINCH

2. BIG, TOUGH BEAK — GROUND FINCH

3. BEAK HOLDING CACTUS SPINE — WOODPECKER FINCH

4. THICK, BROAD BEAK — CACTUS GROUND FINCH

A. SEEDS AND NUTS

B. FRUIT AND FLOWER BUDS

C. BEETLES AND GRUBS

D. LEAF-EATING INSECTS

Then the penny finally dropped for Darwin. He reckoned these fussy finches must all have come from the same ancestor which arrived on the islands years ago. But gradually, they'd each changed their beaks a bit so they could live on different diets. That way there was less competition for food and all the finches were well fed. It was the same with the tortoises. Their different-shaped shells allowed them to reach plants high up or low down. Pretty clever, eh?

Darwin returned to England in 1836 and settled down to write all about his trip. And that's when he came up with an earth-shattering idea called evolution. It explains how some animals had the same ancestors but changed very slowly over time. It certainly changed the course of science. But not everyone was wild about the idea. Especially when some of Darwin's friends claimed that horrible humans might have evolved from apes!

Wild island fact file

NAME: Galápagos Islands
LOCATION: Pacific Ocean
SIZE: 8,000 sq km
ISLAND TYPE: Oceanic
LARGEST CITY: Puerto Ayora
POPULATION: about 25,000
WILD FACTS:

• They're a group of 13 main islands, eight smaller islands and 40 tiny islets, about 1,000 kilometres off the west coast of Ecuador.

• They're the tops of underwater volcanoes which are still erupting. The oldest island's about four million years old.

• The name Galápagos comes from a Spanish word for tortoise. So you could say giant reptiles put these far-out islands on the map.

• In 1978, they were turned into a World Heritage site to protect their unique wildlife.

So you've gawped at truck-sized tortoises, had a big, sloppy kiss from a dragon, and ogled at amazing aye-ayes. And you're looking forward to a well-earned rest? No chance. To keep you on your toes, we've kept the wildest of all island animals to last. What are these extraordinary creatures? Why, horrible humans of course. And they're in the next chapter, waiting to meet you…

WILD ISLAND LIVING

All over the world, millions of people live on wild islands. And because there are so many islands, there's a mind-boggling variety of lifestyles. Some islands are so terribly tiny and remote that very few humans live there. But some wild islands are big, bustling countries and home to millions of people. So what's so great about island living? Here's Isla to spill the beans. She's been given a special assignment as the Daily Globe's travel reporter. We've sent her to check out some islands and find out how people live there. Trouble is, she's having such a wild time, we haven't heard a peep out of her. Typical, isn't it? She gets to jet off to far-flung places and you get to be bored rigid at school. It just isn't fair… Oh, hang on, that must be the post.

Wild island lifestyles

Dear Everyone,
Here I am in Samoa, halfway between Hawaii and New Zealand in the South Pacific. This is a group of volcanic islands, with sandy beaches, rocky mountains and thick forests. Lovely. Even though people here have lots of mod cons, many Samoans still live quite traditionally. Take fishing, for example. They get fish and shellfish from the sea, just as they've done for centuries. Though it's easier said than done. The islands are surrounded by razor-sharp coral reefs and treacherous currents. Luckily, the islanders know the sea like the back of their hands. They know exactly where to go to find the best fish, without getting hurt or swept away. They paddle out to sea in dug-out canoes, then use nets, spears and traps to catch the fish.
Love from Isla xxx

The Daily Globe, London, England.

SAMOA

Philippines, Pacific Ocean

Dear Everyone,

Since I got here yesterday, the weather's been dreadful. It's turned seriously wild and windy, and it's raining buckets. Trouble is, these islands lie smack in the path of some of the fiercest storms ON THE PLANET. And about 20 hit the islands each year. In November 2013, they were battered by a terrible typhoon (tropical storm) that turned the isalnders' lives upside down. Typhoon Haiyan was the deadliest typhoon to hit the Philippines EVER. Winds howled at speeds of 285 kilometres per hour, leaving a tragic trail of destruction behind. Whole towns were flattenened or washed away, and millions of people lost their homes. At least 6,300 people died. Call me a weedy wimp but I'm outta here.

Love from Isla xxx

The Daily Globe, London, England

124

Photo of me leaving! ↴

Pitcairn Island, Pacific Ocean

Dear Everyone,

This titchy, volcanic island is stuck miles from anywhere in the South Pacific. Only about 48 people live here and they're horribly hardy and tough. They need to be. The island's so isolated, supplies have to be brought in by boat three times a year. But if the weather's too wild and stormy, the boat can easily run aground on the reef. The boat also brings post for the islanders, so a letter can take months to arrive or leave. It's tough making a living on Pitcairn. The islanders fish and grow crops like sweet potatoes and oranges.

Love from Isla xxx

The Daily Globe,
London,
England.

PITCAIRN

Japan, Pacific Ocean

Dear Everyone,

Japan's made up of about 4,000 islands (though most people live on the four largest). Did you know these wild islands are one of the world's wealthiest countries? With every mod con you could dream of — computers, tablets and even robots — living's easy here in Japan. It doesn't feel like being on an island at all. The cities, where most people live and work, are big and bustling, just like those on the mainland. And you don't feel cut off because island hopping's a cinch. Bridges and tunnels link the main islands and you can hop across by road or rail. The piccy on the front of this postcard shows one of the three bridges that's been built between the islands of Honshu and Shikoku. It's almost 4 kilometres long and it's bridging the gap nicely.

Love from Isla xxx

The Daily Globe, London, England.

HONSHU - SHIKOKU BRIDGE

Wild island fact file

NAME: Japan
LOCATION: Pacific Ocean
SIZE: 377,915 sq km
ISLAND TYPE: Oceanic
CAPITAL CITY: Tokyo
POPULATION: 126.9 million
WILD FACTS:

• Honshu's the largest Japanese island and the seventh biggest island in the world. Over three-quarters of Japanese people live on Honshu.
• About 1,500 earthquakes shake Japan every year.
• The world's longest underwater rail tunnel links the islands of Honshu and Hokkaido. It's 53.85 kilometres long.
• Sushi (raw fish) is a popular dish in Japan. Tonnes of fish and seafood are caught each year off the Japanese coast.

Singapore, Indian Ocean
Dear Everyone,
I've hopped south to Singapore and I'm on the last leg of my journey. Because of its handy location between the Indian and Pacific oceans, this little island's one of the world's busiest ports. Ships from all over the world dock here to load and unload their cargo. Singapore's also an important business centre and this has made the island very rich. Most people here live very comfortable lives and have all the mod cons you can think of. The problem is it's only a small island and it's getting horribly crowded. Space is running out and so more and more skyscrapers are having to be built to make the most of any spare land.
Love from Isla xxx

The
Daily
Globe,
London,
England.

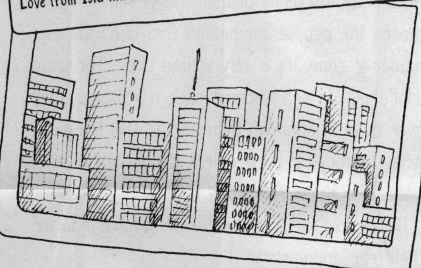

Goodbye, Blasket Islands

As you've seen, on some isolated islands, people still try to live a traditional lifestyle. They live by fishing, farming and raising animals, just as they've done for centuries. But it can be horribly hard to earn a living, especially if the weather turns against you or you start to run out of good farmland. Many people leave their islands to find work on the mainland. And many of them never return. Which means the people left behind find it harder and harder to cope. It's a very vicious circle. For some islanders, life can become such a struggle, they even have to abandon their homes. This is exactly what happened to the people of the blustery Blasket Islands, off the west coast of Ireland.

Here's how the *Daily Globe* might have reported their tear-jerking story:

The Daily Globe

1954, The Blasket Islands, south-west Ireland

ISOLATED ISLANDERS ABANDON HOMES

It was a sad day for the isolated Blasket Islands yesterday when the last islanders left for good. As their boat sailed away, the islanders waved goodbye to the islands that had been their families' homes for generations.

"It breaks my heart," one tearful islander told us. "But I'll never forget these islands – they're in my blood."

Fifty years ago, some 176 people lived on Great Blasket, the largest island. But as the harsh conditions

and terrible weather made life too tough, whole families upped sticks and moved to the mainland. Others headed across the sea to America to start a new life. For those people left behind, it was the beginning of the end.

These wild but beautiful islands lie off the south-west coast of Ireland. For the hardy islanders, life has always been a struggle to survive.

"We didn't have any new-fangled gadgets like telephones," another islander told our reporter. "Our only link with the outside world was by boat. And if the weather was too stormy to make the crossing, we were completely cut off. It was tough luck if you were ill. You had to wait for the weather to clear so the boat could take you to the mainland to see a doctor."

Home for the islanders were stone houses they'd built themselves, with felt roofs covered in thick tar to keep them watertight. Most houses had only two small rooms – a kitchen (with space for dancing and keeping animals at night), and a living room that doubled up as a bedroom. There were just a few pieces of furniture, mostly made from driftwood washed up on the beach. And there was no running water or electricity, mod cons most of us take for granted these days. Instead, the islanders collected water from the well, and dug up turf and heather to burn on the fire. The firewood was bundled on to the back of a donkey to take home because the islanders didn't have any cars or tractors.

Finding enough to eat was another problem facing the islanders. With no shops on the islands, the islanders had to rely on the land and sea for food. But it wasn't always easy.

"We grew a few crops – some potatoes, oats and vegetables," one islander told us. "Some of us kept a cow or two, and a few sheep. And we hunted for rabbits on the hill. But most of our food came from the sea. We took our little boats out and caught pilchards, lobsters and crab. And very tasty they were, too. If the weather was good, there were rich pickings to be had. But if it turned too wild and windy, well, we just went hungry. Simple as that."

Despite the harsh conditions, the islanders still found time to enjoy themselves. They loved to spend evenings dancing to fiddle music and singing songs. And there were always hundreds of stories to tell, like the time when a chest full of tea washed ashore and the islanders had their first cup of tea! However tough their lives have been, these proud and hardy people will miss their island homes terribly. But so many people had already gone that only the old and young were left. And this made it impossible for the island community to survive for much longer.

Could you be an island castaway?

Think you're tough enough to live on an isolated island? Try this quick quiz to find out. The most important question is how on Earth are you going to survive? Apart from wild and windy weather, there are plenty of horrible hazards about. Forget a refreshing paddle in the sea or lounging about in the sun. Being a real-life castaway is NO PICNIC. Have you got what it takes to stay alive?

```
┌ ─ ─ ─ ─ ─ ─ ─ ─ ─ ─ ─ ┐
│        IMPORTANT NOTE:         │
│ By the way, we're not sending you to a nice, │ ◯
│ cushy island with loads of mod cons. That would │
│ be much too easy. Nope. We're leaving you all │
│ alone on a wild island in the middle of nowhere │
│ with nothing and no one else for miles around. │
│ Still keen to give it a go? │
└ ─ ─ ─ ─ ─ ─ ─ ─ ─ ─ ─ ┘ ◯
```

1 You're marooned on your desert island and you're gasping for a drink. Trouble is, even though you're surrounded by water, it's so salty it'll make you sick. How on Earth can you quench your thirst?

a) Dig a deep hole in the ground.

b) Hope it rains – and soon.

c) Drink your own pee.

2 Oh dear, talking of water, it's begun to pour with rain. You've built yourself a driftwood hut but you haven't quite finished it in time. What can you use to make a waterproof roof?

a) Dried seaweed.

b) Palm fronds.

c) Seashells.

3 What's that strange noise? Sounds a bit like thunder? Oh no, it's your tummy rumbling. All that hard work's made you peckish, but what is there to eat? You've heard roast octopus is quite tasty. But how do you make sure an octopus doesn't give you the slip?

a) Shake a coconut-shell rattle at it.

b) Set an octopus-hunting shark on it.

c) Catch it in a rat-trap.

4 Oops! That was a close shave. A coconut falls off a tree and narrowly misses your head. Luckily you kept it (the coconut, as well as your head). But what on Earth can you use your new-found nut for?

a) Keeping things in.

b) Keeping clean.

c) A tasty snack.

A RATHER NICE HAT

5 You've been on your island for weeks now, with only your pet octopus for company. (Yep, we noticed you wimped out of eating it.) And you're desperate for someone to talk to. How can you make a quick getaway?

a) Swim for it.

b) Build a canoe.

c) Wait for a ship to find you.

ANSWER

1 a) You could go without food for several weeks but without water you'd be dead in three days or less. So make the most of a downpour and stock up on rainwater to drink. (Make sure you strain it first to get rid of any bugs.)

If the sky's clear and blue without a rain cloud in sight, you could try digging a (very) deep hole to get at any underground water. But dig your hole well away from the beach, otherwise the water will still be salty. As for drinking your own pee, that will just make you thirstier.

2 b) On most desert islands, there are palm trees galore. So find a handy palm tree and break off some of the fronds, or leaves. Split each one down the middle, then lay them flat on the roof. Make sure they overlap neatly to keep the rain out. It's best to build your hut slightly raised off the ground. This'll keep you safe from creepy-crawlies and other crafty creatures like rats and snakes.

But leave the sides open. That way, if a typhoon strikes, your hut's less likely to blow away.

3 c) To tempt your lunch out of its hole on the coral reef, you need to make an octopus trap.

Here's what you do:

• Take a smallish rock.

• Wrap it in leaves and bits of hairy coconut shell to make it look like a rat. (OK, so you'll have to use your imagination for this bit.)

THAT'S THE WORST RAT I'VE EVER SEEN

• Dangle your rat-trap in front of the hole.

• When the octopus sneaks out to take a look, reel the rat-trap in and grab the octopus by its tentacles.

Easy, peasy, eh? By the way, the coconut-shell rattle doesn't work on octopuses but you could use it to stun a shark. First, shake your rattle in the sea to attract the shark's attention. Then you can snap the shark up. If it doesn't snap you up first.

SHARK BURGERS FOR TEA!

4 a), b) and **c)**. Yep, you can use it for all three. If you run out of insect repellent, rub on coconut oil instead. It's brilliant for keeping pesky mozzies away. But that's not all the oil's good for. If you run out of soap (remember soap?), you can use it to wash behind your ears. And, of course, the white insides of a coconut are delicious to eat. You can even eat the little beetles that live on your coconut if you fancy something crunchy to munch for lunch. Why not try some with your octopus? But mind their little legs and wings don't get stuck in your teeth.

5 b) The best way to get off your island is by dug-out canoe. Hop into one of these and you'll be in good company – islanders have been using them for centuries to get from A to B. But with no handy shops around, you'll have to make your own canoe. Think you're up for that? OK, here's what you do. Cut down a tree trunk and hollow out the middle with a knife or axe. Put a couple of planks inside for seats and make a paddle from a piece of wood. Simple, isn't it? Well, you'd better get going – you could be paddling for days. Be careful you don't capsize – there are bound to be some rattled sharks about.

Now add up your score...

Give yourself ten points for each correct answer.

Score 50: CONGRATULATIONS! You'd make a brilliant castaway. You've stayed alive against all the odds and you haven't got homesick once.

Score 30–40: Although you've had a wild old time, you've still got a lot to learn. For a start, you can't keep everything you catch as a pet. Or you'll starve to death. Oh OK, the octopus can stay.

Score 0–20: You won't last long as a castaway. You're just not tough enough. Better stick to staying at home instead. Then you won't get bashed on the nut by a coconut.

Earth-shattering fact

Depending on where your wild island is, it might not be easy to leave. Take the tiny, volcanic island of St Helena in the middle of the Atlantic Ocean. It's remote and horribly rocky, with sheer cliffs plunging into the sea. And there'd be no point trying to swim for it – its nearest neighbours are on Ascension Island over 1,000 kilometres away. Imagine being cast away there! All of which makes it the perfect spot for an ... escape-proof prison. Yep, from 1815 to 1821, St Helena was home to one of the most famous prisoners in history – the fiery French general, Napoleon Bonaparte. Bet he was wild about that.

Worn out by all this wild living? Seen enough islands to last you a lifetime and keen to settle down for a while? Don't worry. We've found a new victim, sorry, volunteer to take your place for a while. So while you enjoy a well-earned rest, wave goodbye to your brave old geography teacher. He's about to set off on the journey of a lifetime. And he'll be in good company. Once the intrepid explorers in the next chapter get going, there's no stopping them.

ISLAND HOPPING

People have been exploring wild islands for centuries. Of course, some of them didn't do it deliberately. I mean, if you found yourself shipwrecked, even the most isolated island might look quite homely. But other people planned their journeys more carefully. They set off to find new islands to live on when things got a bit crowded back home. Some explorers were in it for money.

145

They were on the look-out for goods to trade. And others simply wanted to run away to sea and have a wild old time. Some island explorers only had a short hop to get themselves from A to B. But others had to cover vast stretches of ocean without knowing exactly where on Earth they'd end up. Think your teacher will be able to keep up?

Meandering monks

In the early 6th century a meandering monk, St Brendan (born AD 484), set out from Ireland on an extraordinary voyage. He wanted to find the beautiful 'Promised Land of the Saints' which legend said was an idyllic island far away to the west. Trouble is no one knew exactly where. First plucky Brendan had to cross the Atlantic Ocean and woe betide him if he got lost. Unlike modern sailors, he didn't have any maps or mod cons to help him find his way. And his ship was no high-tech sailing machine. Oh no. This intrepid explorer set off in a tiny boat made from leather, stretched over a wooden frame. The leather was smeared with dollops of fat to keep it nice and watertight! Hopefully. Here's a map of the island-hopping route we think brave St Brendan took:

GREENLAND

7 Crossing more treacherous and stormy seas, the monks sailed around the south coast of Greenland, keeping clear of the glaciers. Luckily for them, the weather was slightly warmer in those days so there wasn't so much ice about. Unluckily, it was still bloomin' f-f-f-freezing.

8 They were now on the last leg of their journey, heading west. Soon they reached a mysterious island, half hidden by thick mist and fog. When the clouds cleared, the monks found a beautiful place, full of fruit trees, flowers and babbling brooks. You get the picture. After seven years' island-hopping, they'd reached the Land of the Saints at last. (Horrible geographers reckon this island might have been Newfoundland, off the coast of Canada in North America.)

NEWFOUNDLAND

9 But the weary monks didn't have long to relax and take in the scenery. It was soon time to turn their boat round and head back home to Ireland. Fancy going all that way for a bit of peace and quiet!

6 Soon afterwards, they came to a rocky island. But they didn't dare get too close. The whole place seemed to be on fire and the wild islanders pelted them with red-hot rocks. They were outta there sharpish. (Horrible geographers reckon this island was fiery Iceland and what the monks saw was a violent volcanic eruption.)

ICELAND

5 Leaving the Faroes, the monks turned west to cross the icy ArcticSea. It wasn't all plain sailing. They were chased by a savage sea monster which foamed at the mouth. (It was probably the wild whale.) And they were dazzled by a pillar of sparkling crystal rising from the sea (which was probably an awesome iceberg).

FAROE ISLANDS

4 The next island was oddly grey and bare, with no grass or trees in sight. Legend goes the hungry monks went ashore, lit a fire and began to cook their lunch. Imagine their astonishment when their island began to swim away! It seems they'd actually landed on the back of a whopping whale which had just woken up from its morning nap!

3 Heading further north, the monks' next stop was a pair of isolated islands they called the Island of Sheep and the Island of Birds. You can guess how they got their names. (Horrible geographers think these islands were in fact the Faroes.)

2 Heading north, they sailed up the west coast of Scotland where a terrible wind whipped up. The boat was blown onto a high, rocky island. (Horrible geographers think it might have been one of the Hebrides.)

IRELAND

1 With 14 fellow monks, St Brendan left Ireland on his quest for the Land of the Saints. There wasn't room for much luggage, just a change of woollen clothes, a bit of spare leather for patching, water in leather bottles and supplies of food for the first 40 days.

*It's said St Brendan could see into the future. So he knew exactly where he was going and what he'd find at every step of the way. Without having to use a muddlesome map. How handy would that be on holiday?

Earth-shattering fact

Ask your geography teacher who discovered North America and she's bound to say, "Christopher Columbus in 1492. Anyone knows that." But is your teacher right? What if St Brendan got there first, **OVER A THOUSAND YEARS EARLIER?** In 1976, intrepid British explorer, Tim Severin, set out to retrace St Brendan's route. He wanted to see if a bunch of mild-mannered monks could really have sailed across the awesome Atlantic and reached Newfoundland in a little leather boat. Did he make it? Yep, he did. Though luckily for Columbus, there's no real proof that St Brendan managed it.

Treasure islands

I FEEL A BIT PECKISH!

THE BUZZARD

As well as stopping-off points for adventurous monks, wild islands also made perfect hideaways for perilous pirates. Or, more importantly, for perilous pirate treasure. And of all the plundering pirates to roam the high seas, dashing Frenchman Olivier Levasseur (1690–1730) was one of the bloodthirstiest. Nicknamed "The Buzzard", he thought nothing of capturing passing merchant ships, cruelly killing the crew and making off with all the lovely loot. Gruesome, eh? Oddly enough, young Olly did well at school and his favourite subjects were ancient history and astronomy (the study of the stars). But he soon got bored of lessons and went off to become a pirate superstar instead.

For years, the bloodthirsty Buzzard terrorized ships in

the Caribbean Sea. Then he headed for the Indian Ocean where he'd heard there were rich pickings to be had. And, sure enough, his luck was in. One fine day, he came across the rotting wreck of a treasure ship that had run aground in a terrible storm. And guess what? It was jam-packed with gold and silver bars, chests crammed with gold coins, precious pearls and diamonds, sumptuous silks and works of art. The gob-smacked Buzzard couldn't believe his eyes. He wasn't just fantastically wealthy. He was rich beyond his wildest dreams!

But there was also a price on his handsome head. In case he was captured, he needed to find a fool-proof place to bury his treasure. And he needed to find it fast. So where did our filthy-rich pirate pick? There might be a clue in his secret diary. If you dare to sneak a peek. (Don't blame me if you get caught.)

MY TOP-SECRET DIARY
BY ZEE BUZZARD (ZAT'S ME)
KEEP OUT- ON PAIN OF DEATH
(P.S. I MEAN IT.)

SCARY, HUH?

WHAT A FANTASTIC DAY IT'S BEEN! GUESS WHAT? I ONLY CAPTURED A TOP TREASURE SHIP AND NOW I'M FILTHY RICH! IT WAS CRAMMED FULL OF GOLD AND SILVER AND DIAMONDS, AND POTS AND POTS OF DOSH. OH I'M RICH! I'M RICH! I'M RICH! (AND EVER SO HANDSOME AND DASHING!)

IT WAS SOOO EXCITING. OF COURSE, I FOUGHT QUITE BRILLIANTLY. THEY DON'T CALL ME ZE BUZZARD FOR NOTHING, YOU KNOW. I SWOOPED DOWN ON THE SHIP AND GRABBED THE TREASURE, JUST LIKE A . ER, BUZZARD. BUT I MUSTN'T GET CARRIED AWAY.

I NEED SOMEWHERE NICE AND SAFE TO STASH MY LOVELY LOOT. HMM, LET ME SINK . AH, YES, I GOT IT. I'LL BURY IT ON THE ISLAND OF MAHE IN THE SEYCHELLES. I FANCY A BIT OF A HOLIDAY. ZERE'S A LITTLE SPOT THERE CALLED ██████ JUST BY THE ROCKS AND DOWN A BIT FROM THE ████████.

EDITOR'S NOTE: SORRY, THESE BITS ARE TOO SMUDGY TO READ.

ZAT'LL DO NICELY. THEY'LL NEVER FIND IT ZERE. NOT IN A MILLION YEARS. HEE! HEE! HEE!

THEN, WHEN I'VE FINISHED PLUNDERING, I'LL GO BACK AND GET IT. AND BLOW THE LOT ON PREZZIES FOR... ME!

Unfortunately for the boastful Buzzard, his luck ran out soon afterwards. He was captured and tried for piracy, found guilty and sentenced to death by hanging. So he never got to go on his shopping spree. But this surprising pirate had one last trick up his sleeve. As he was led to the gallows, he tossed a piece of paper into the crowd and shouted: "Find my treasure, if you can."

Imagine what you'd do with all that money! You could buy all the latest CDs and computer games. And have a new pair of trainers for every day of the week. Without having to save up your pocket money. But there's just one teeny snag with this get-rich-quick scheme. First you have to find the treasure. Can you make head or tail of the Buzzard's baffling treasure map?

154

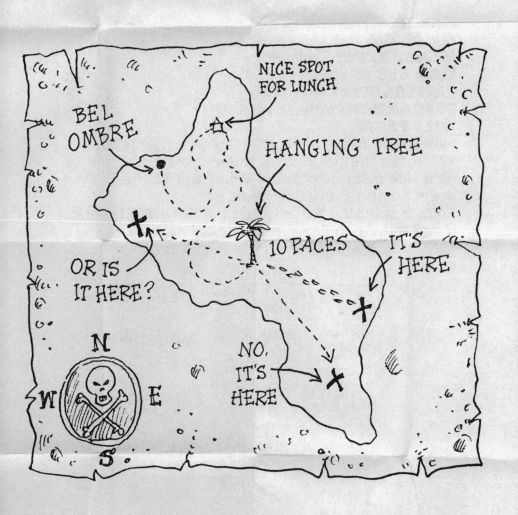

155

Wild island fact file

NAME: Seychelles
LOCATION: Indian Ocean
ISLAND TYPE: Continental
SIZE: 455 sq km
CAPITAL CITY: Victoria
POPULATION: around 92,430
WILD FACTS:
• They're an archipelago of about 115 islands.
• They're the peaks of a huge, drowned chunk of land left behind by India when the plates drifted apart about 65 million years ago.
• Their stunning scenery and palm-fringed beaches make them popular places for holidays.
• No one lived on the Seychelles until the 18th century.

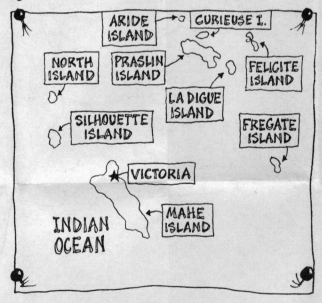

People are still digging up bits of the Seychelles in the hope of finding the Buzzard's buried treasure. Among them was retired British soldier, Reginald Cruise-Wilkins whose search lasted over 30 years. Reginald reckoned some mysterious markings on the rocks were clues to the treasure's whereabouts. He spent thousands of pounds on equipment and dug loads of pits and tunnels underground. But sadly, apart from an odd coin or two, he didn't find a thing. Me? Oh, I'm glad you asked. I'm, er, just doing a spot of, hem, gardening.

Long-lost islands

Even if disappointed Reg didn't dig up any dosh, at least the island itself was still there. Which is more than can be said of Atlantis, a legendary island that's been lost for centuries. Where on Earth was Atlantis? And how come it vanished without trace? No one really knows. Plenty of people tried to track it down and failed miserably. So we decided to bring in top detective, Chief Inspector Wilde, to investigate. If anyone could find this mysterious, missing island, he was the man for the job. If you want to find out how he did, here's the Chief Inspector's private case notes for you to read…

THE CASE OF THE MISSING ISLAND

It was the toughest case I'd taken on. Sure, I've tracked down plenty of missing humans but this was my first missing island. Clearly this was no ordinary case. So I decided to hit the secret police files to find out exactly what I was up against. It was easier said than done. Atlantis was last seen thousands of years ago so the files were pretty battered and old. And the dust really got up my nose. Aaattchhoo!

Anyway, as I read on, one man's name kept cropping up, and I hoped he'd give me a lead. His name was Plato and he was an Ancient Greek. I wanted to bring him in for questioning but unfortunately he was dead. Long dead. Luckily, I had a copy of the statement he'd made at the time. Here goes…

According to this Plato, Atlantis was a rich and powerful island with fabulous palaces and beautiful scenery. It sounded sensational to me. Its king commanded a huge army and ruled over a vast empire. (Of course, Plato had never actually been there so it was all just hearsay.) Until one fateful day, that is, when this incredible island sank beneath the waves. Without trace. It wasn't much to go on, I know, but it was all I had. So I had my assistant draw up a missing island poster based on what we knew so far. This is what he came up with:

MISSING!

HAVE YOU SEEN THIS ISLAND?

NAME: ATLANTIS

LAST KNOWN ADDRESS:

NOT KNOWN. POSSIBLY SOMEWHERE IN THE ATLANTIC. OR THE PACIFIC. OR THE MED.

DISTINGUISHING FEATURES:

A LARGE-ISH, ROUND ISLAND WITH ITS CAPITAL CITY BUILT ON A HILL. THE KING LIVED IN A LUXURIOUS PALACE ON TOP OF THE HILL. A HUGE CANAL LINKED THE CITY TO THE SEA. AND THAT'S IT, I'M AFRAID.

REWARD OFFERED FOR SAFE RETURN

But it turned out to be a long shot. We had copies pinned up everywhere but no one got in touch. With no eyewitnesses or evidence, the trail went horribly cold. We didn't even have a scene of crime to visit. I began to think I'd made a big mistake taking on this crackpot case. The whole thing was hopeless. Talk about a wild-goose chase. Wild, no, I wasn't wild. If you must know, I was bloomin' livid.

Where on Earth was Atlantis?

So Atlantis had our top cop well and truly stumped. Perhaps you can solve the mystery. Don't worry if you don't know the answer. Just have a wild guess. Which of these wild islands would you pick as the most likely suspect?

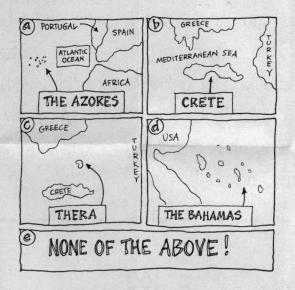

a) Definitely not. Some people thought the Azores in the Atlantic were the tops of freaky peaks left behind when Atlantis sunk. But geographers now know they're violent volcanoes which have burst up from the sea floor.

b) It's possible. Crete's one of the Greek islands in the sunny Mediterranean. Just like Atlantis, a mighty civilization grew up there thousands of years ago. And it met a sticky end when it was destroyed by an earth-shattering earthquake. But, unlike Atlantis, this wild island didn't sink into the sea. Which is good news for the thousands of holiday-makers who visit it every year.

c) It's possible. Thera's another Greek island, quite close to Crete. In about 1450 bc, this violent volcano erupted, blowing most of the island away. So could it be Atlantis? Some scientists think so. They've found the ruins of a great city buried under the volcanic ash and reckon Thera and Atlantis are one and the same place.

d) It's unlikely. In 1968 divers found hundreds of huge stone blocks under the sea off the Bahamas. But what on Earth were they? And how did they get there? Could they be the ruins of a temple from Atlantis or part of an ancient road? Scientists don't think so. They say the stones are natural and have nothing to do with long-lost islands.

e) The most likely explanation. Never mind about going missing, expert geographers say, there's no proof that Atlantis ever existed in the first place. Plato probably made the whole thing up. But, of course, even experts don't know everything. Perhaps the ruins of Atlantis are still lurking under the sea, just waiting to be found. What do you think?

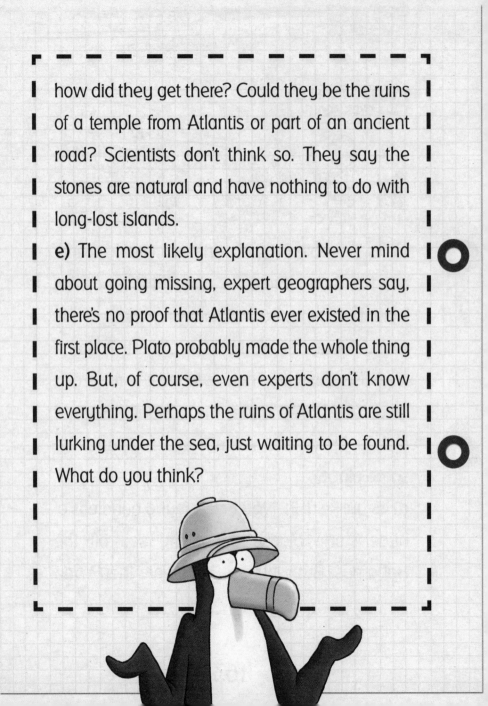

TEACHER TEASER

Oh dear. The dog's really eaten your homework this time and you daren't tell your teacher. While you work out what to do, distract her attention with this tasty question.

PLEASE, MISS, DOES BREAD GROW ON TREES?

Are you a sandwich short of a picnic?

ANSWER

Bread does grow on trees. Well, sort of. At least, breadfruit do. Never heard of them? They're green fruit about the size of footballs. You can use them in lots of recipes and they're cheap and easy to grow. In fact, you could say they're the best thing since, well, sliced bread. In the 18th century, some rich but mean London bigwigs hatched a cunning, penny-pinching plan. They sent a ship, the *Bounty*, to the Pacific island of Tahiti to collect some breadfruit plants. The ship was to take the plants to the West Indies as cheap food for the bigwigs' slaves. So in 1787, the *Bounty* set off with Captain Bligh and his crew on board. But it wasn't a happy ship. By the time they left Tahiti in April 1789, the bickering had reached fever pitch and first-mate Fletcher Christian led a mutiny. He chucked the breadfruit overboard and cast the captain and a few loyal sailors adrift in a tiny boat.

But the mutineers weren't safe yet. They needed to find a hideaway, somewhere so secret and isolated they wouldn't get caught and punished. And they found the perfect place – lonely Pitcairn Island, a tiny, rugged island just 5 square kilometres in size. It was years before they were found. Most of the islanders who still live there today are descended from the mutineers. So you see, the whole thing wasn't completely fruitless after all.

HE LOOKS JUST LIKE HIS GREAT-GREAT- GREAT- GREAT GRANDFATHER

Paddling Polynesians

People went to live on Pitcairn Island to get away from it all. But teeny-weeny Pitcairn's just a drop in the ocean. What about the thousands of other isolated islands flung far and wide across the Pacific? How on Earth did the ancestors of today's islanders get there? Take Polynesia, for example. For years, the question of where the Polynesian people had come from had horrible geographers well and truly stumped.

Polynesia means 'many islands' and it certainly lives up to its name. It's a triangular group of about 25,000 islands in the south Pacific. The three points of the triangle are Hawaii (in the north), New Zealand (in the south) and Easter Island (in the east). Some of the islands are high and hilly. Others are low-lying coral atolls. Getting hopelessly lost? Here's Isla with a handy map to help you get your bearings.

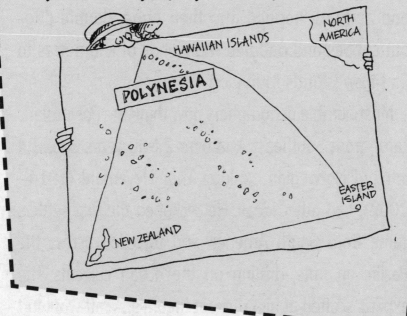

169

Crossing the Pacific ... by raft

The plucky Polynesians were born sailors. Long before anyone from Europe had even heard of the Pacific, they were busy exploring it. And their journeys were carefuly planned. When things got too crowded back home, they packed up their plants and animals, hopped into their huge, double dug-out canoes and paddled thousands of kilometres to find new islands to live on.

Most horrible geographers now think the Polynesians came from Southeast Asia over 2,000 years ago. But intrepid Norwegian explorer, Thor Heyerdahl (1914–2002), had other ideas. He reckoned the first settlers came from South America and travelled across the Pacific on rafts, drifting on the ocean currents. The experts scoffed at his crackpot theories. A raft wouldn't stand a chance, they said. Even if it didn't sink, you'd be washed overboard. But tough-nut Thor didn't care what the experts thought. And he set out to prove them wrong. Did he sink or swim? Here's how the *Daily Globe* might have reported his treacherous trip.

The Daily Globe

TUAMOTU ISLANDS, POLYNESIA

AUGUST 1947

Top Norwegian explorer Thor Heyerdahl was relaxing today on the sunny Tuamotu Islands while he celebrated the end of an epic voyage. Over three months ago, he and five courageous companions left Callao on the coast of Peru in their flimsy balsa-wood raft, Kon-Tiki. Their remarkable journey ended a few days ago when the Kon-Tiki ran aground on a coral reef.

A beaming Heyerdahl was thrilled to have made it this far. "The experts said we'd never make it," he told our reporter. "And I wanted to prove them wrong. Now I've done it and I'm over the moon!"

Building a raft
Heyerdahl and his team spent months in Peru, building their remarkable raft. It was an exact copy

of the rafts used by ancient South American sailors and every detail had to be just right. Finding the balsa wood for the boat turned out to be one of the hardest parts.

"Unfortunately, this was easier said than done," Heyerdahl told us. "We could buy lots of balsa wood but not in the form of whole logs. Then we were told that the only place where large trees grew was in the thickest part of the jungle. Getting those logs was a really hard slog."

But they finally got the nine huge logs they needed and lashed them together to make a raft. It had a bamboo deck, a tiny cabin, sails and an oar for steering. Then they stocked the raft with supplies. The ancient South Americans most likely lived on sweet potatoes and dried llama meat. But Thor relied on army rations instead.

Oddly enough, these included 684 boxes of pineapples.

Across the Pacific

At last, on 28 April, the raft was ready to be launched. It was christened with coconut milk and officially named Kon-Tiki, after an ancient Peruvian sun god. For Heyerdahl and his five-man crew, it was the last time they'd see land for weeks. Between them and their destination lay almost 7,000 kilometres of wide open sea.

For the next 101 days, the raft drifted west on the currents while the men battled with giant waves, killer sharks and slippery swarms of jellyfish.

On one occasion, they were followed by a huge (but harmless) whale shark which could easily have tipped the raft up. Their only shelter was the tiny bamboo cabin and they were always soaking wet. But worse was to come. About halfway through their journey, they ran into a violent storm. Tonnes of water poured on deck and one man fell overboard. (Luckily, he was later found alive and well.) But there was no doubt they were dicing with death.

Land ahoy!

On 30 July, they finally caught their first sight of land. An island lay in the distance. But their excitement was short-lived. Trouble was, between them and the island lay a treacherous coral reef. Despite their best efforts, the wind whipped up and blew them straight towards the razor-sharp reef. As the going got rougher, the men braced themselves. Heyerdahl described their crash landing:

"We must have hit the reef," he said. "The sea thundered on, over and past, and as it roared by it revealed a terrible sight. The Kon-Tiki was completely changed, as if by a magic wand. The vessel we knew from weeks and months at sea was no more. In a few seconds our pleasant world had become a shattered wreck."

The men were battered and bruised but luckily none of them was badly hurt. And as they got their bearings, they realized they were stranded on a tiny desert island which Heyerdahl described as "heavenly". Above all, they'd achieved the impossible. They'd sailed across the Pacific on a raft and proved even expert geographers can get things horribly wrong.

So how did your teacher get on without you? Will he be back in time for double geography, or is he still having trouble steering his canoe in a straight line? Of course, compared with what ancient sailors had to go through, modern island hopping is a doddle. All you have to do is hop on board a boat or plane and you're there in no time at all. But if you still haven't found your ideal island hideaway, you'd better hurry up. Wild islands all over the world are going under fast.

ISLANDS IN DANGER

It's official. Despite the risk of typhoons, shipwrecks and volcanic eruptions, horrible humans are wild about islands. But are islands quite so wild about them? Islands might look rock solid but don't be fooled by appearances. Because many islands are so small and isolated, they're far more fragile than they seem.

Terrible tourists

Each year, millions of globetrotting tourists head for islands all over the world. Sunny weather, warm seas and sandy beaches make places like the Caribbean and Greek islands the perfect spots for a summer holiday. But with more and more visitors every year, these islands are feeling the strain. Looking forward to your next island-hopping holiday? You might want to think again.

HORRIBLE HOLIDAYS ARE **NOT** PROUD TO PRESENT THEIR LATEST REVOLTING RESORT...

WELCOME TO
WHAT-A-MESS ISLAND

FOR A HOLIDAY YOU'LL WANT TO FORGET

We can't guarantee you'll enjoy your stay. But if your holiday's ruined, you've only yourself to blame. Come to think of it, you might want to change your mind and stay at home this year instead!

HARMFUL HOTELS:

While you're relaxing in your room, think about how your hotel got there. With more holidaymakers, more hotels need to be built. (Not to mention roads and airports.) So miles of coastline are concreted over to make building space, and beaches and coral reefs are mined for materials.

WAT-ER PONG!

What could be better than a day at the beach, messing about in the sea. But whose mess are you swimming in? Horrible humans are making the sea sick by pumping sewage straight into it. Disgusting but true. And more tourists means, yep, you've guessed it, even more waste to wash away. Still keen to make a splash?

THIRSTY WORK:

You've spent the morning sunbathing and you're ready for a refreshing drink. But if you want a glass of water, you might be in for a long wait. On many small islands, the water supply is rapidly running out. Too little rain's one reason. But awesome amounts of water are also being used for holiday hotels, swimming pools and golf courses.

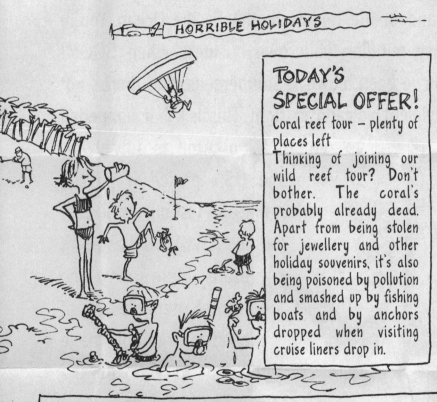

HORRIBLE HOLIDAYS

TODAY'S SPECIAL OFFER!

Coral reef tour – plenty of places left

Thinking of joining our wild reef tour? Don't bother. The coral's probably already dead. Apart from being stolen for jewellery and other holiday souvenirs, it's also being poisoned by pollution and smashed up by fishing boats and by anchors dropped when visiting cruise liners drop in.

A NOTE FROM YOUR TOUR OPERATOR:

The trouble is, many small islands rely on tourism to make a living. Too many tourists spoil the islands, but if the islands get messed up, it'll stop the tourists coming! It's a horribly vicious circle.

Going up with a bang

One of the perils of being isolated is you're horribly easy to pick on. Picture the scene. You're a tiny coral island in the middle of the Pacific Ocean. You're busy minding your own business when BOOM! You've been blown to smithereens. And there's not a violent volcano in sight. This is what happened to remote Bikini Atoll in July 1946 when the USA picked it as the perfect place to test out its nuclear bombs. With devastating results. Here's how the earth-shattering events of that time might have appeared to one of the shell-shocked islanders.

My story by Joji

I remember it like it was yesterday although I was only ten years old at the time. You see it turned our lives upside down and things still aren't back to normal. To be honest, I don't think they ever will be. Our nightmare started in March 1946. There were 168 of us on the island at that time. Our families had lived there for generations. We were told we had to move to another island so our island could be used for testing nuclear bombs. We weren't really sure what it all meant and besides, what could we do about it? We were just a few ordinary people living on a tiny island. Anyway, they dropped the bombs a few months later. I remember seeing the enormous mushroom-shaped cloud. It was a truly terrible sight. Somehow I knew I'd probably never see my beautiful home again.

After that, we were never in one place for long. We were moved from island to island, until we finally ended up on Kili Atoll, 800 kilometres from home. Life on the island was desperate. For a start, there was no lagoon for fishing and no harbour for our boats. Quite often we went hungry because the land was too rocky to farm. Meanwhile, more and more bombs were being tested.

Anyway, time went by and about 20 years later, we were told it was safe to go home. At last. It seemed too good to be true. Some families moved back at once but most of us were too scared to go. You see, the bombs had released deadly radioactive waves that can burn your skin and cause killer diseases like cancer. And we didn't want to take the risk. Later, we found out we'd been right not to go. The radioactive waves poisoned the water supply and the soil was still full of deadly chemicals so we wouldn't have been able to grow any crops. The people who'd moved back were moved on again. There was nothing else for it.

And things still haven't changed. I'm an old man now and I'd do anything to see my home again. But I don't know if it will ever happen — at least not in my lifetime. And that makes me very sad.

As if having your island home blasted by deadly rays wasn't awful enough, some unfortunate islanders are facing another appalling problem. Their isolated islands are in serious danger of sinking.

Wild island fact file

NAME: The Maldives
LOCATION: Indian Ocean
SIZE: 298 sq km
ISLAND TYPE: Oceanic
CAPITAL CITY: Malé
POPULATION: 393,253
WILD FACTS:
• They're a group of about 1,800 coral islands in the Indian Ocean.
• The islands are so low-lying, none of them poke up more than 2 metres above the sea.
• People only live on 202 of the islands. Some of the other islands have been turned into holiday resorts just for tourists.
• Most people live by fishing and working in the tourist hotels. About 1.2 million tourists visit the Maldives each year.

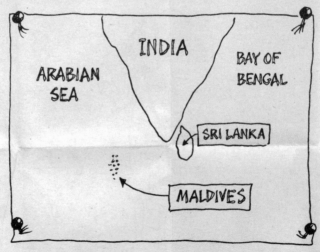

That sinking feeling

With their crystal clear lagoons and sandy beaches, the Maldive islands are ideal holiday hideaways. But if you're planning a visit, you'd better get your skates on. Sadly, these wild islands may not be around for much longer. And the bad news is that horrible humans are to blame. Why? Well, we're making the Earth too bloomin' hot. Scientists call this global warming and you might think it would be a bonus, especially for a holiday hot-spot. But in fact, it could spell disaster. Here's a horrible weather warning...

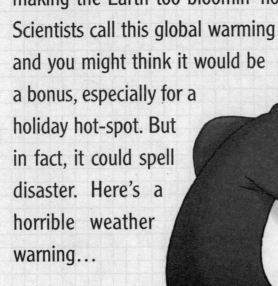

1 Horrible humans are pumping tonnes of gases like carbon dioxide into the atmosphere. It comes from …

… cars …

… and factories …

… and from burning forest trees.

(It's also the stuff you breathe out.)

2 These ghastly gases act like an enormous blanket wrapped around the Earth. It traps the heat coming from the sun and keeps the Earth toasty warm.

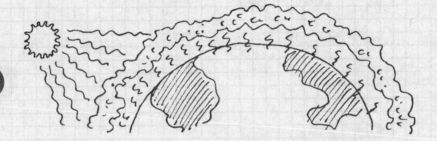

3 But it also stops some of the spare heat escaping and this is making the Earth horribly hot. And that spells trouble.

4 If the Earth gets too hot, it could melt the ice sheets and glaciers at the perishing poles ...

5 ... making the sea level rise and drowning low-lying islands like the Maldives.

The enterprising islanders built a sea wall around the capital city, Malé, that protects it if the sea starts to flood in. And, for years, they've been campaigning to stop global warming. But it's horribly slow going. And they're running out of time. Already the shoreline's crumbling. In fact, the ground's disappearing beneath their feet. And the rising salt water's killing their crops and poisoning the water supply.

Scientists can't agree how long the islands will last. But they guess the whole Earth will heat up by about 2°C by the year 2100. This could melt enough ice to make the sea level about 50 centimetres higher. Which doesn't sound much but the sea only needs to rise twice that much to swallow the islands up. And that would be a terrible tragedy.

A wild future?

But you'll be glad to know, it isn't all doom and gloom. The good news is people are working hard to save the world's wild islands. Already some islands are being turned into national parks to protect their weird wildlife. Remember the incredible Galápagos Islands? Only a limited number of tourists are allowed to visit the islands today and they can only go with a guide. So the island's amazing animals get left in peace and quiet.

Earth-shattering fact

It's true, some islands are sinking. But as some islands go under, others are springing up. And these wild islands are nothing to do with violent volcanoes or cracking continents.

Yep, artificial islands are all the rage. The world's biggest artificial island has been built on the coast of Dubai in the Arabian Gulf. It looks like a giant palm tree, complete with a giant trunk and fronds. It has been turned into a posh holiday resort, with loads of luxury villas, shops, cinemas and theme parks. Fancy a holiday hideaway on Palm Island? You'll need to save up your pocket money. A villa with its own private beach and swimming pool could set you back a cool £60 million!

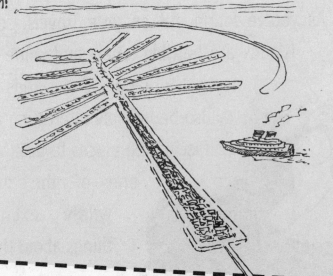

So, you're back safe and sound after your incredible island-hopping adventure. Hopefully you've found your dream island hideaway and you're feeling wonderfully refreshed and relaxed. Sadly, your nice, warm glow doesn't last for very long. What a welcome home it's been! Your mum's already nagging you to tidy your room and your little brother's nicked your brand-new trainers. No wonder you're already planning your next intrepid trip. As you've found out on your travels, some islands are horribly lonely and some are too hot to handle. But islands can also be horribly interesting and fascinating places to visit. And one of the most wildly exciting things about them is that you never quite know who or what you'll bump into next...

HORRIBLE INDEX

FOR MORE HORRIBLE
ADVENTURES, EXPLORE
THESE BOOKS!

HORRIBLE GEOGRAPHY

NEW EDITION

BLOOMIN'
Rainforests

ANITA GANERI
Illustrated by MIKE PHILLIPS

HORRIBLE GEOGRAPHY

NEW EDITION

PERISHING
Poles

ANITA GANERI
Illustrated by **MIKE PHILLIPS**

HORRIBLE GEOGRAPHY

NEW EDITION

ODIOUS
Oceans

ANITA GANERI
Illustrated by MIKE PHILLIPS